SOCIAL SKILLS FOR KIDS

How to Build Confidence, Strong Communication Skills, and Become Your Best Self

Jamie Myers

ISBN: 978-1-957590-29-5

For questions, email: Support@AwesomeReads.org

Please consider writing a review!

Just visit: AwesomeReads.org/review

FREE BONUS

SCAN TO GET OUR NEXT BOOK FOR FREE!

TABLE OF CONTENTS

Chapter Six: Negotiation & Problem-Solving Skills 62

Chapter Seven: Responsibility Skills 74

INTRODUCTION

As humans, most of us are constantly exposed to various social situations—at school, on social media, among family or peers, and out in the community. Sometimes, it can be difficult to know how best to handle these situations.

By learning essential social skills like self-control, communication, empathy, and active listening, you will begin to understand how to respond to most social situations without fear. You may even find that you begin to approach them with excitement.

Having these skills will benefit you in various ways. Social skills may help you make and keep friends, reduce your stress levels, perform better in school, and form deeper and long-lasting relationships with the people around you.

This book will teach you the social skills you'll need both now and later in life, including:

- Communication
- Cooperation
- Active listening
- Respect
- Engagement
- Responsibility
- Empathy
- Self-control
- Problem-solving

We've also included activities in each chapter that will help you practice the lessons you're learning. Through this practice, you'll develop stronger social skills, which can help you to feel more confident in any situation.

On that note, let's get started!

CHAPTER ONE:

ALL ABOUT SOCIAL SKILLS

In this chapter, we'll look at social skills and why they're so important for you, both now and in the future.

You'll also learn when some of these abilities begin to emerge for many people. We don't expect infants to have a strong sense of responsibility! By thinking about the times when some of these skills may start to come more naturally for you, it may become easier to apply them in the situations you encounter.

This chapter will also identify some factors that can affect social development and explain when it's a good idea to seek help with a particular challenge.

WHAT ARE SOCIAL SKILLS?

Social skills are the skills we use to communicate with and relate to other people. They make up the different qualities and abilities that help us get along with others—our classmates, teachers, parents, and everyone we interact with.

As humans, we are social beings. As a species, we tend to rely on others and to value forming relationships with those around us. Of course, some people may be described as more outgoing than others, and some may really enjoy their solitude. But relatively speaking, compared with other species, humans are very social

Behaviors like smiling, waiting your turn, and sharing what you have are all usually friendly — these are friendly social skills. Being able to interpret others' emotions — like knowing that your friend feels sad just by looking at them — is another skill that is very important. Having this awareness of others' feelings can make them feel valued, and if they're sad, that alone can help them feel better.

This book will cover some key social skills — including forms of both verbal and nonverbal communication — that will be valuable to you as you build, strengthen, and maintain relationships with your family, friends, teachers, and acquaintances. Remember that practice is always key to building new skills, so make sure you take advantage of the practice activities throughout this book.

WHEN DO KIDS DEVELOP SOCIAL SKILLS?

While babies aren't born with what we think of as *skills*, we all enter this world knowing how to communicate. Newborn babies cry instinctively and soon begin using their voices to express their needs, such as food or comfort.

In the days and weeks that follow, babies begin to make eye contact with others, use different sounds to express different feelings, and even smile at familiar faces. Even from the very beginning of your life, you were learning and using social skills.

As you grew older, you probably began interact with people other than close family members. For example, maybe you went to a preschool or a play group where you could interact with other kids your age.

When this happened, you began to need new and different social skills. You needed to learn how to get along with your peers and teachers, not just your parents and siblings.

4

And that's not where it ends. As you continue to grow, you'll keep learning new skills. These skills will help you throughout the stages of your life, and you will continuously be learning new skills, or improving the ones you have.

So don't worry if you don't yet have all the skills we will discuss in this book, or if some of them feel hard for you to learn. It just may not be time for it yet. That might be a skill that will come at another time for you.

Let's take a look at some of the stages young children go through, and the social skills associated with those stages. Remember that everyone is different. The examples listed below might not be totally true for you. These are general examples based on groups of people, but every individual's experience might be different.

Ages 0–3 years:

At these ages, your life revolved around your close family members. As such, you learned most of what you knew, including social skills, from them.

During this time, you began your first attempts at communicating. You cried when you were uncomfortable and smiled when you were happy.

You also started to recognize familiar faces from a very young age. For example, as a toddler, you probably smiled at parents or close family members but felt a bit more hesitant with strangers.

These were also the ages you began to interact with others by sharing your toys and playing with — or at least alongside — other kids. As a toddler, you probably began to express yourself with stronger emotions. For example, maybe you fought with a sibling over toys or had a temper tantrum when you didn't get your own way.

That behavior can be intense and difficult to be around, but it's perfectly normal for young children learning to communicate their feelings. The bright side of these ages is that you were becoming constantly more social—building strong bonds with your family and probably beginning to make some friends, using your imagination while playing, and even beginning to understand the feelings of others.

At these young ages, you probably enjoyed receiving praise from people around you. Communication is not only about a person's ability to express themselves, but also responding appropriately to others around them. So, at this time, you realized that praise or playing with a friend could bring you good feelings.

Ages 3–5 years:

You may have attended childcare or preschool during this time, or maybe you were at home with family or a babysitter. It's likely that you initially found it hard or stressful to be away from your parents, but most young children gradually adapt and get used to being a bit more independent for periods of time during the day.

Most children are quite interested in others at this age. It becomes easier for children to play together, make friends, and learn how to be a part of a group.

As kids develop a better sense of self-control during this time, they may find it easier to express their feelings and control really extreme behavior. You may have started to find it easier to share or wait your turn, and maybe those temper tantrums became a bit less frequent as you got better at communicating your needs in calmer ways.

Ages 5–7 years:

You probably have more memories of these ages than the ones that came before.

As you entered the school-age years, your independence grew, and you likely began actively pursuing new friendships.

While your parents or family were still the most important people in your life, friends started to become more important than they had been before. You may have started to become friends with kids who liked to do the same activities as you, or who had the same interests. It's also likely that some of your friends were simply the kids who lived closest to you, or those who were in your class. A lot of our friendships are based on how frequently we see other people.

At this age, you also began to better control your impulses, cooperate with others, and follow instructions, even when an adult wasn't present. In addition, you got better at resolving disagreements with your friends without an adult getting involved.

Ages 7–9 years:

Around these ages, social situations may start to become a bit more complicated. Many people become more aware of and sensitive to others' opinions around these ages, and as your feelings start to become somewhat more mature, they might feel confusing. It may sometimes feel difficult to find the right words to express your emotions, which can be an uncomfortable feeling in itself, but it is normal.

Children around this age may start to develop closer friendships, or sometimes even have someone who feels like a "best" friend.

This can be a fun time for communication, as kids develop their sense of humor further and enjoy telling jokes.

By this time, many children are able to write, and that adds a new element to communication, as well. You might have been able to write notes or text messages to your friends around this age, where prior to this time, all of your communication would have been in words or behaviors.

Ages 9-12 years:

During the preteen years, you may become even more self-aware and discover things about yourself you didn't know before. You'll also begin to experience the emotional changes that come with puberty, which can be a struggle to manage and control at times.

It's during this time that peer pressure may start to play a bigger role in kids' social lives. Peer pressure may involve communication tactics like persuasion, negotiation, being assertive, compromise, and more. While these are all terrific skills to develop in general, the increasingly complex social relationships of the preteen years can be a hard time to try to figure all of this out.

If you are feeling misunderstood, hurt, or confused, find a trusted adult with whom you can discuss your feelings.

On the flip side, at these ages, you may start to move towards self-acceptance, developing more positive self-esteem and self-assurance. Your friendships may become very close, and your family relationships may deepen as well, as you're able to communicate more clearly about more mature topics. Socially, the preteen years will be very rewarding, which will hopefully help to balance out some of the challenges of these years.

WHERE DO KIDS DEVELOP SOCIAL SKILLS?

So, we've discussed a very general timeline for when some social skills begin to emerge on average, but let's explore further the where. Where do you develop social skills?

At Home

The home is generally the first place you begin to develop your early social skills, and your home will continue to be a crucial part of your social development throughout your life. You learn social skills by watching how your parents and family members behave and interact. At first, you'll tend to copy what you see them do. Over time, what you learn and observe in the home will contribute to the development of your own unique social skills and style.

With Other Children

As you play with other children, you learn vital social skills like sharing, how to follow directions, cooperation, taking turns, and kindness. Playing with others also helps you better understand your emotions, feel proud of your achievements, and develop a sense of who you are.

At School

At school, you benefit from both adult guidance and influence from your peers. Here, you learn about respect and authority. In addition, you learn teamwork, how to kindly and respectfully work out differences, and much more. As you grow older, you might have to work with other children on a project, which is a great chance to practice your communication, cooperation, and teamwork while being creative with others.

In the Community

When you are out and about—maybe attending church, accompanying your parents on errands, or enjoying your favorite restaurants and community locations—you have many chances to observe how older children and adults talk, work, and play with each other. It's in your community that you learn how to interact with unfamiliar people. Over time, you will get a sense for how to respond in different or unfamiliar situations.

A NOTE ON DEVELOPMENT

It is so important to always remember that not everyone grows at the same rate. Different kids develop different social skills at different times, and that's okay.

It's normal for social situations to feel difficult, for emotions to feel confusing, or for communication to feel complicated at times. Often, the times when it feels the hardest are the times when you're actually learning the most. So be patient with yourself.

If you find that you're struggling with your social skills, or have any concerns, always find a trusted adult to talk to about your worries. They might be able to reassure you, or they might offer some suggestions for how you could work on the things that are feeling difficult.

WHY IS IT IMPORTANT FOR KIDS TO LEARN GOOD SOCIAL SKILLS?

Social skills are important for everybody to learn and practice, both young and old. As we've discussed already, childhood is a time when this learning can happen very quickly. Kids learn a lot in a short amount of time. But you'll keep learning throughout your life.

Solid social skills — the ability to express your feelings and needs, collaborate with others, and show respect and kindness — are crucial to society functioning.

Imagine a world where these skills don't exist. What would happen if people never waited their turn? If people always lied to get what they wanted? Or always just blurted out the first things that popped into our heads?

It would be utter chaos! All of these scenarios would cause frustration, hurt feelings, and lots of disappointment. Social skills are what help us live and work together with others in peace and kindness.

In addition, learning good social skills at a young age may have a positive impact on your health and happiness throughout your life.

For one, social skills enable you to connect with other people and build friendships and relationships. This, in turn, enables you to cope with loneliness and stress and boosts your self-esteem.

Having good social skills will also be helpful in your future jobs, and in your future interactions with your community. Being able to cooperate, motivate others, and resolve conflicts with other people will be part of your life on a regular basis. All of these things would be difficult or impossible without strong social skills.

So, given the significance of social skills, it's important that you learn a wide variety of appropriate words, behaviors, and actions. These skills include empathy, communication, friendship, respect, problem-solving, self-control, and many more.

Now let's look at each of these skills, their importance, and how you can develop them.

CHAPTER TWO:

COMMUNICATION SKILLS

Communication is something everyone does, every day. You communicate with your family, friends, teachers, strangers, and even your pets. Everyone has their own way of communicating. Babies communicate by crying. Older people communicate through speech, writing, behavior, and sign language. Even animals communicate.

WHAT IS COMMUNICATION?

Communication means sharing information. But it isn't just sharing information. It involves sharing information that other people can understand through listening, speaking, paying attention, and asking questions.

In relating to others, we use many different methods to pass information and share our thoughts and feelings. Sometimes, we use verbal communication (speech), while other times we use nonverbal communication like gestures, body language, and facial expressions.

This means you may still be communicating even when you're not saying anything. For instance, an adult could scold you by folding their arms, or a person could express their anger by slamming a door. Other people may be able to interpret your thoughts or feelings by what you do, even when you don't say any words. Through nonverbal communication, our actions send a message.

13

Because we communicate through both verbal and nonverbal communication, strong social skills are dependent on both language and also behavior. They'll help you send the right message and stop you from sending the wrong one.

Communication can also be written. Books, websites, letters, and magazines are channels of written communication. Communication can also be done visually using graphs, charts, and maps.

Here are a few examples of times you communicate:

When you lift your hand in class—this communicates that you want to speak.

When you ask a question in class or at home—this communicates that you want more information.

When you are telling your friend about a place you visited during the holiday or you listen to their story. Both speaking and listening are forms of communication.

When you are hurt, and you cry. Crying is a way to communicate that you are in pain or you're not comfortable.

When you go to the store to buy candy, you tell the storekeeper what you want, and they let you know if it's available or not. You and the storekeeper are both communicating with one another.

WHY ARE COMMUNICATION SKILLS IMPORTANT?

Everything you do in life involves communication. As long as you meet people daily, you will communicate every day. You won't be able to share your ideas or learn from others if you don't know how to communicate.

Communication will make things easier for you. Learning good communication skills will help if you want people to understand you when you speak or act a certain way.

Imagine that you're hurt and are crying, but nobody understands what's going on with you. Maybe instead of asking you what's wrong, someone tells you to stop making noise. Of course, you would feel really bad because the person doesn't understand that you're hurt. This is why communication is necessary, so that we can understand each other.

There are many reasons why communication skills are essential. Here are some of these reasons:

#1 Communication Skills Help You Express Yourself Better

Everybody wants to be able to explain how they feel to others. When we aren't able to explain how we feel, it can sometimes make us feel even worse. We might start to feel lonely in addition to feeling sad. If you can communicate effectively, you will be able to explain your feelings and problems to others, which might help you solve them.

#2 Communication Skills Will Help You Make Friends

Strong communication skills help us to get along well with others and are important in building and maintaining our friendships and other relationships. Generally, people who can express themselves find it easy to interact with others, even if they are strangers.

One of the greatest things that keeps a friendship going is communication. If you learn to communicate well, you're sure to not only make friends, but you'll also be able to keep those friendships strong.

#3 Communication Skills Will Help You in Your Career as an Adult

Everyone in a workplace must communicate regularly — through speech, writing, and body language. There are few jobs that don't require regular, ongoing communication.

Even if you prefer being alone, at times you still need to interact with others while working. You're probably learning this already from your class projects, presentations, or other school events. Collaborating, cooperating, brainstorming with others, and working on a shared project are all important communication skills you are practicing in school and which will be important to your work life later on.

Good communication skills are very important for a successful career. This means that if you want to do well in your chosen profession, you need communication skills.

#4 Communication Skills Help to Prevent Disputes

If you have good communication skills, it means that you understand others when they speak, and others can understand you when you talk as well.

This will help you pass on information clearly and help others understand you quickly. People listen more to those they can understand easily, and this helps to prevent misunderstandings, disputes, and frustration.

#5 Communication Skills Help You Become Confident

When you learn good communication skills, you may find that people are more willing to listen to you. This will boost your sense of confidence and self-esteem and could help ease some fears. For example, many people get nervous about speaking in public or making presentations. The stronger your communication skills become, the more confident you may feel in these situations.

HOW TO EXPRESS YOURSELF WITH WORDS

The ability to use words is a very important aspect of verbal and written communication. Knowing how to express yourself with words determines whether you can pass on your intended message or whether your listener may feel confused, frustrated, or even hurt by what you are trying to say.

Here are some tips to help your communication when it comes to the use of words:

#1 Know the Right Words to Use

Using the appropriate words is an important part of communication. There are certain words that you can only use in an informal setting. This means you use those words when you are speaking to family and friends that you are close to or other people that you already know well.

The way you speak to your friends will be different from how you talk to a stranger. Also, the way you address your parents will be different from how you address other adults like your teachers or principal.

You can ask your parents to tell you words that are appropriate to use when speaking to other adults. This starts with how you address them. For example, it's inappropriate to start a conversation with an adult by saying, "Hey!" Instead, you can say, "Good morning, Mr. Smith," or, "Hello, Miss Julie."

#2 Don't Ramble

Rambling means saying too many words at once without a break for the other person to speak, and especially if you talk for a long time without making a clear main point. Try to convey your message without using too many words when you are speaking. Instead, learn to get straight to your main point. This is a skill that can take some practice.

Rambling may cause your listeners (or readers, if you are rambling while writing) to be confused about the main point of what you're trying to say, simply because you're saying too many things. When this happens, people may just tune out because they've lost interest in what you are saying.

#3 Speak Respectfully

Whether you are speaking to an older person or your peers, proper communication skills involve respecting their points of view. One way to show your respect is through your use of words.

Even if you disagree with what someone is saying, don't respond by saying things like, "What you just said is stupid...it makes no sense." You must acknowledge and try to understand others' points of view before trying to convince them of your own views. Remember, there is always something you can learn from other people, so listen carefully to see what they have to share with you.

Let your words show that you respect other people's opinions. You can say, "I understand what you're trying to say, but I don't think it applies to this situation," or, "Your points are valid, but I think we can also do it this way..."

When you do this, people will feel better because they will know that you have paid attention to what they have to say. They will also be pleasant to you, and this will help you have more honest and productive conversations.

#4 Ask Questions

Asking questions will help you get clarity on things that you don't understand. Asking questions also makes people feel better about talking to you because they feel you're interested in what they have to say.

When you ask good questions, you're also sure to gain more details and knowledge about the subject you are discussing.

WAITING BEFORE RESPONDING

We often think of communication as being mostly about what we put out—what we say or write to others. But always remember that communication also involves what you take in. In other words, an essential aspect of good communication skills is being a good listener. Listening is a very important part of communication. Some people want to keep talking and never listen to other people's views. But such a conversation is one-sided, and one-sided conversations are neither enjoyable nor productive. Communication involves both speaking and listening to others.

Take your time while listening to others. Try to keep your focus on the person who is speaking, and remember that you don't need to respond immediately. It's actually a good idea to wait a moment before responding. Waiting before responding is important because:

It gives you time to process what you heard to ensure that you understood it. For example, if someone asked you a question, make sure you think about and fully understand the question before trying to answer it.

It helps you give the right response. When you correctly understand a question or statement, you can give the answer that's appropriate for the situation.

It helps you to take charge of your emotions. If you're angry or upset about something you've heard, you should likely wait before you respond to it. Waiting helps you to cool off so you don't say something you may regret or that may hurt the other person. This applies equally in writing. Maybe you read a message from someone and it hurt your feelings or made you angry. Take some time to think rather than responding immediately, so you can avoid overreacting or making a situation worse.

It gives you a chance to actually focus on the person and the topic, especially if the conversation has become emotional or frustrating.

CONTROLLING YOUR EMOTIONS

Another element of communication skills is learning to control your emotions. If you are in a conversation that is heated, or that has made you angry or frustrated, a good way to control your emotions is by taking a break from the conversation. You might do this by stepping away from the person and taking a walk to cool off.

If the conversation is with an older person, it would be impolite to just walk away from them, especially while they are still speaking. Instead, a way to control your emotions is to take a deep breath and keep silent while they talk. Try to calm down and not respond or cut in while they're still speaking.

You may even say, "Please can I have some time to think about this and give a response later?" It's almost always appropriate and a sign of maturity to be able to ask for that time, saying something like, "I feel angry about this right now and maybe it would be better if we talk about it tomorrow when we're both calmer."

If given a chance, you can even choose to give your response in writing. When you write out your answers, you're often better able to arrange your thoughts and use words correctly. If you give in to your anger and write things that are rude, you have the chance to go back and read what you wrote before sending it, to make sure you're being intentional with your response.

Sometimes you don't have the opportunity to physically step away for a break, or to give a response in writing. For example, if your teacher has asked you a question, you'll need to respond then and there. But it's still okay to collect your thoughts before speaking. Practice counting to ten before you give a response.

Counting in your mind may help to keep your emotions in check and help you think through the situation before you answer.

LEARNING THE DIFFERENCE BETWEEN PUBLIC AND PRIVATE CONVERSATIONS

Private conversations are conversations that are personal, confidential, and only involve a particular group of people. The extent of the privacy often depends on the people and topics involved.

A conversation between your parents in their bedroom is a private conversation and, as a child, you are not to eavesdrop on such conversations. If they wanted it to be public, they would talk about it at the dinner table when you're all together.

A private conversation can also be one that you and your friend have without others around. The idea of privacy means that the conversation is only meant for certain people to hear, and not everyone is welcome or appropriate to join it. For example, if you are talking with your teacher about your grade on a test, you would not want the whole class to participate in that conversation. It's only appropriate for you and the teacher to discuss.

A public conversation is the exact opposite. With public conversations, the conversation is open. Anyone can join it, the content of the conversation is not meant to be secret, and it often happens in a general or exposed setting.

A good communication skill is the ability to know the difference between private and public conversations. For instance, if you want to talk to your friend about something they did that you didn't like or that hurt your feelings, you should find a place where there aren't many people around to have that talk. Maybe your room, or a secluded part of the playground or class.

Don't have private conversations in places where many people are likely to overhear the conversation or eavesdrop on it. You can speak in low tones if you don't have a private place to speak. If the conversation is likely to make you or your friend upset, then you want to do it in a place where you won't be interrupted by others.

On the other hand, if you're chatting with a friend about a TV show you both watched last night, you could do that in any public setting — walking down the hall, on the playground, or in the cafeteria — without worrying about others hearing.

ACTIVITIES

To summarize, here are some activities that might help you communicate better:

Practice waiting for ten seconds before responding to others when you are upset. You can record the outcome of the conversation in your journal.

Make a list of conversations that are private, and a list of public conversations. Then write down ideas of places where you could hold private conversations when you want to.

CHAPTER THREE:

LISTENING SKILLS

Listening skills? Listening is an actual skill? It's easy to think that as long as you are able to hear what someone else is saying, that's the same as actually listening.

But in fact, listening goes well beyond simply hearing. Listening means that not only do you hear what someone is saying, you're also paying close attention to what is being said because you want to understand.

Listening is an important social skill—you need it every day because words and sounds are all around us. You need to be able to listen effectively at home, in school, in class, while playing outside, and everywhere you go. Listening helps you communicate better.

So, let's learn about active listening and how you can get better at it. You'll be glad you did.

WHAT IS ACTIVE LISTENING?

Active listening simply means paying full attention to someone or something, and showing them that you are paying attention. It's not just about hearing the words or sounds. It means you're listening to what is being said, word for word, and your mind is set on understanding or remembering it.

When you're listening actively, you will want to show that you're doing so. This is the "active" part of active listening. This might mean making small sounds of comprehension or interest while someone is speaking, like softly saying, "yes" or "ohh" or "interesting." Other behaviors of active listening include nodding, asking questions, sitting up straight, and making eye contact with the speaker.

For example, think about when you are in class and your teacher is explaining a lesson. You might be listening to your teacher, but if you are staring out the window or doodling in your notebook while listening, then this is not active listening. As a result, your teacher doesn't know that you're listening and they could interpret your behavior as ignoring them, being rude, or not being a responsible student.

If you aren't actively listening, you're passively listening. Passive listening means you're hearing but not paying attention — you're distracted. What usually happens in this case is that you miss out on a lot of things that are being said or you find it hard to understand.

On the other hand, if you're listening to the lesson while sitting up straight, nodding, and making eye contact with the teacher, then you are active listening. Your teacher will know you're listening, and will be pleased with your concentration.

Not only is this better for your learning, but it's also much more respectful to your teacher. Nobody likes to give a presentation to an audience who seems bored.

When you're listening actively, don't let yourself get distracted. The fly passing by isn't that interesting. There's nothing attractive about the stain on your jeans, so you don't need to stare at it. What matters at that time is the person talking and what they're saying.

One of the best ways to show you are listening actively is by asking questions and participating in the discussion. You will learn more this way and the person speaking will enjoy talking to you.

WHY ARE LISTENING SKILLS IMPORTANT?

We've looked at active listening and how you can listen actively, but you may still be wondering why you need to listen, or why listening skills are so important in general.

Being a better listener does you a lot of good. Here are some of the benefits:

Better Understanding:

With good listening skills, you can understand information better.

This is because, by actively listening, you pay attention to what is being said without getting distracted. How can you understand anything if you're not even paying attention?

So, if you're finding a subject in school hard or difficult, it could be that your confusion is due to not actively listening in class.

Alertness:

Listening skills help you be more aware of your surroundings. You become able to recognize different sounds better. And this, in turn, can help you tell when something is not quite right. In this way, active listening can contribute to your safety. For example, if you're alert and listening actively, you'll recognize the sound of traffic coming or a crossing guard calling to you.

Better Communication:

Have you ever seen how information can change when passed from one person to another?

There is a game called Telephone, where people stand in a circle. One person starts by whispering a sentence into the ear of the person next to them. That person then whispers the sentence to the person next to them, and so on around the circle. By the time the sentence makes its way around the whole circle from person to person and arrives back at the person who started it, it can be amazing how much the sentence has changed along the journey!

For example, the first person might have said, "We have a white guitar." But by the time it gets all the way around the circle, it's turned into, "We have to hide the car." This doesn't happen on purpose. It's because people don't always speak clearly or listen carefully, so the message is misunderstood as it's passed along.

When you listen more, you'll be able to pass along information more accurately and speak more clearly and intelligently. This might not be the most fun in a game of Telephone, but it will definitely be helpful in your real life.

Clearer Memory:

Paying attention or active listening also helps you remember things better. As you already know, our minds are easily distracted by many different thoughts. As a result, information can get all jumbled up.

However, when you listen actively, you silence other thoughts, enabling you to listen better and remember things more.

And when you have a good memory, you're more capable and can do better in your studies.

Problem-solving:

A good listener can solve problems better. Because your mind is attentive and active to the present topic or problem, you're able to offer a solution.

Also, if the solution has been taught or explained in the past, an active listener will remember it.

Good listening skills help you gather knowledge on many useful things that will come in handy for solving future problems.

Good Character:

Everyone likes those who listen to them when they speak. Good listeners are often seen as caring and well behaved. On the other hand, you're likely to think a person who doesn't pay attention to you is rude and uncaring.

This means that listening skills are part of showing that you have a good character. They also show commitment, respect, and care—all traits of a good leader. Most often, a good leader is a good listener.

Trust:

Adults find that it's easier and safer to trust you with responsibilities when they know you listen. This is because they trust you'll do what they said, the way it was said.

HOW TO BE A GOOD LISTENER

You've seen how important active listening skills are. The next question is, how can you become one?

First, be thoughtful about paying attention to someone who is speaking. It makes the person you're listening to feel good about themselves and what they are saying.

To help you along, here are a few things you can do to be a good listener.

Maintain Eye Contact:

Looking directly at the speaker helps you concentrate on what they're saying. By maintaining eye contact with whoever is speaking, you can give them your full attention and understand what they're saying.

Also, eye contact makes them feel they can rely on you and that you are interested in what they have to say. And in the same way, you won't get distracted by other things.

Don't Interrupt:

When someone is speaking, try not to interrupt them. Let them finish their sentences and if it seems they're pausing so you can speak, then speak or ask a question. Don't attempt to finish their sentences for them or get them to finish quickly.

That only tells the other person you're not very interested in what they have to say.

Ask Questions:

Asking questions is a way to show that you're listening and want to have a clear understanding of what's being said.

Use Nonverbal Signs:

Nonverbal signs like nodding, showing expressions of surprise, agreement, care, etc., show that you are listening attentively.

Repeat What Was Said:

Summarizing what you heard in your own words shows that you were paying attention and understanding what the speaker said. It also helps you remember better what you heard.

So, after listening to something, briefly repeat what you heard. For example, your friend might tell a long story about something that happened at home with their brother, and then their parents yelled at them, and now your friend is angry at their brother and their parents. You don't need to repeat or summarize the whole story. But you can briefly repeat this to show that you've been listening by saying something like, "Wow, that sounds really upsetting. I can tell you're angry at your parents and your brother because of what happened. What do you think you'll do now?" This is a good response because you've expressed your care, showed that you were listening, and also asked them a follow-up question.

REMEMBERING THINGS ABOUT OTHERS

You know that feeling you get when someone remembers a little thing you mentioned in passing? Did it make you feel seen and important? If so, you're not alone in that. We all feel that way when others remember things about us.

However, there's no way you can remember anything about anyone if you weren't listening to them in the first place. This is another reason you need good listening skills.

Here are a few things you can do to remember things about others:

Pay attention to the person: You should care enough to note a special feature about the person. It could be the tone of their voice, a mark, their hair, or even their clothes. Remembering a visual cue like this can help you to also remember the content of the conversation you had with this person.

Pay attention to the environment: Try to link people with events or places. That way, when an event comes to mind, you'll remember the person around that event or location. Even smells and fragrances can remind you of a person or situation. For instance, the smell of freshly baked cookies may remind you of a time you were playing a game with your grandmother.

Repeat a person's name: When you learn a new person's name, you should repeat it aloud immediately to help your memory. So after they introduce themselves, try to say their name in your greeting, such as, "Hi, Mark, nice to meet you."

Go over your day: Learn to go over your day and try to remember specific things that happened. Then, talk about it with your parents, siblings, or friends. Retelling the story of an event can help to reinforce the parts that you want to remember.

ESSENTIAL LISTENING SITUATIONS

Some situations need more attention than others. So, you want to make sure you're listening during those times. Here are a few examples:

Directions: No one likes getting lost. To avoid this, make sure you're paying attention when directions are given.

Class: Everything that happens in class requires attention and recollection. Listening will help you be a better student which will in turn make you a more clever and more careful adult.

Medical Situations: If you are visiting the doctor or dentist, you'll need to pay careful attention and listen actively throughout the visit. Anything your doctor or dentist says is likely to be relevant to your health and well-being, and you'll want to remember it.

In an Unfamiliar Situation: Listening is very important when you're in a place you've never been before. Maybe you and your family are traveling to a new city. Or maybe you just started a new club and are attending the first meeting. If the location and other people are unfamiliar to you, make sure you're paying close attention to what is going on so that you can figure out how to stay safe, avoid getting lost, and start to participate in what is happening around you.

ACTIVITIES

Learning to listen can be fun. It doesn't have to be boring or a chore. This is why we've put together some activities you can do to help you become a better listener.

Treasure Hunt:

A fun game to play while developing important skills is a treasure hunt. Treasure hunts require lots of attention because in each phase of the treasure hunt there are tasks, riddles, and puzzles with clues to follow.

If you want to find the treasure, then you can't be distracted when you're being told the clues or riddles. So channel your inner Jack Sparrow and learn to listen while you're at it.

Story Creating:

Another fun game to play is to create a story with your friends, classmates, or family. Get everyone in a circle and begin a story. Then everyone has to contribute a part to the story.

This way everyone has to listen to each person in order to contribute in a way that flows with the story. It's a great game to build listening skills.

The Telephone Game:

This is the game we described above, and it requires a group of people (at least six). Get everyone together in a circle. Whisper a phrase or word to the next person who must also whisper what they hear to the next person.

Each person whispers to the next person until you've come full circle. At the end of the game, each person should say what they heard. You'll see how well everyone listened, and how easily information gets lost or mixed up along the way.

CHAPTER FOUR:

FRIENDSHIP SKILLS

As we've said before, human beings are social creatures. This means that even from a young age, we tend to want to relate with the people around us. This leads us to develop friendships.

But being able to easily make friends or be a good friend are not skills we're all just naturally born with. Some people can make friends easily, while others may be good at other things but find it difficult to make friends.

In this chapter, we'll focus on friendship skills, why these skills are essential, and how you can learn to make and keep good friends.

If you don't have the skills to make friends, we'll teach you how to do this. And if you're already a natural when making friends, still read along—you may learn something new.

This chapter will also cover how to use social media positively, and other topics. There's a lot to learn and improve on.

Let's dive right in!

WHAT ARE FRIENDSHIP SKILLS?

Before we get into what friendship skills are, let's first define what friendship is.

Friendship is a relationship that involves two or more people who share mutual affection and bonding. Friends spend time together, confide in one another, and have each other's back. As such, friendship gives you a sense of belonging.

However, friendship requires reciprocity. This means that for any relationship to be a friendship, you and your friends must like each other. You can show this reciprocity in simple ways like sharing your lunch, exchanging books and toys, and playing together.

Now, to friendship skills. Friendship skills have to do with the ability to make and keep friends. People use them to build and maintain personal relationships that involve shared interests, mutual affection, and bonding.

If you find it difficult to make friends, don't worry. You can learn to build your friendship skills. Thankfully, there are various activities that you can engage in to help you learn important friendship skills.

You can learn to get along with others and enjoy their company with the right amount of practice.

WHY ARE FRIENDSHIP SKILLS IMPORTANT?

Friendship skills are essential for many reasons. If you can make and keep friends, you will enjoy several benefits that will impact you positively. These benefits include:

#1 Emotional Development

The right friendship skills are essential to the social and emotional development of children like you.

Friendship skills—learning to be sensitive to others, sharing with others, and learning the rules of conversation—are life skills. These types of skills are good for our emotional and physical health.

The truth is that every child feels the need to be accepted, especially among their peers. When you have friends, it gives you a sense of belonging, and it boosts your self-esteem, happiness, and confidence. It helps you feel secure and be as productive as possible.

Knowing how to make and maintain friendships will also give you a more positive outlook on life. It may help to relieve times of stress and intense emotion.

#2 Better Communication

Having friendship skills will also help you communicate more effectively and efficiently. The more you interact with other kids your age, the better you'll get at communication.

You will learn important communication skills like knowing how to express yourself so that others understand you. Also, friendship skills will help you to listen to others when they speak so that you can understand what they're trying to say.

#3 Impacts on Your Future

If you have good friendship skills, you're more likely to be successful as an adult than other kids who don't know how to be friendly. With friendship skills you can build, maintain, and grow meaningful relationships.

This will really help you in the future when you have a career or business, get married, or find yourself in other social situations.

HOW TO MAKE FRIENDS

There are different skills that you'll need if you want to learn how to make and maintain friendships. But to learn how to make friends, you must first understand the importance of qualities like sharing with others, listening to others, respecting their opinions, showing kindness, and apologizing.

Here are some things you can do to make it easy for you to make friends:

#1 Make a Good First Impression

A first impression is what a person thinks of you the very first time they see or meet you. Many people believe that first impressions are lasting impressions. This isn't necessarily true (we also know we can't judge a book by its cover!) but it's still a good idea to make a good first impression on others when you can.

Do you know that it only takes seconds for a person to form a perception of who you are when they see you? In those few seconds, the person is asking themselves, "Do I want to know this person better? Are they worth spending time with?"

Your ability to make a good first impression may make it easier to get to know others and start to make friends. Don't worry; making a good first impression doesn't have to be hard. Just follow the tips given below.

A good first impression can be based on many different things. There's no one way to make a good impression on others. Everyone is different! So, what one person might perceive as really funny, charming behavior might come across to someone else as kind of annoying. There's no way to guarantee that you'll make a good impression on every single person you meet, and you still want to be yourself.

The tips below are some general ideas to keep in mind that will help you make a good impression regardless of who you meet, while still being true to yourself and your own personality.

Hygiene: Most people respond well to good hygiene, and have a more negative response to poor hygiene. So make sure the clothes you're putting on each day are clean, and that you shower or bathe regularly. Brush your teeth and wash your hands. Avoid habits like biting your nails, especially in public.

Attitude: Having a generally polite, respectful, and friendly attitude is appropriate in every situation. Practice making eye contact when someone is speaking to you, and greeting others with a smile. Even if you're having a bad day, strangers don't need to get involved in that, so try not to pout or be rude when meeting someone new. They still deserve your respect and kindness, even when you're having a bad day.

Conversation: It might be hard to talk with people you don't know, especially if you tend to be shy or an introvert. You don't need to try to be the life of the party. But make sure that you do say hello and introduce yourself to people, and even make some small talk if you can, asking questions like, "How long have you lived here?" or commenting on the weather. The more you practice making basic conversation and communicating with new people, the easier it will become.

#2 Having a Conversation:

This involves factors like making pleasantries, introducing yourself appropriately, asking appropriate questions, and using appropriate language.

There are basic greeting phrases used to greet different people. For instance, when you're familiar with someone you can say, "Hi, how are you?" On the other hand, you can approach an unfamiliar person by saying, "Hi, I'm Sophie. I live on the next block. What's your name?"

Like other skills, practice will do most of the work. Practice starting conversations with your family members at home. You can also practice starting a conversation in front of a mirror by yourself.

Learn how to make small talk, especially when you meet someone with similar interests. Ask questions and focus on the answers the other person gives.

Additionally, avoid turnoffs in conversations like excessive teasing, using rude words, or speaking so much that others don't have a chance to participate. Don't ask people overly personal or private questions about themselves or their families.

#3 Cluing in to the Moods of Others

This means identifying a person's mood and interpreting their body language. Cluing in to other people's moods is also a vital friend-making skill.

There are certain verbal and nonverbal clues that can enable you to determine a person's mood. For instance, if a person fails to respond or stops contributing to a conversation, it may signify that the person has lost interest in it.

Also, cues like yawning, rolling eyes, and tapping of feet may indicate boredom and a desire to end the conversation.

If you find yourself in a conversation with such a person, what do you do? You have options. You can try ending the conversation or pausing so that the other person has an opportunity to say something.

There are also certain appropriate responses to specific moods. For example, teasing a person when they're crying is improper. Instead, you can ask questions like, "Is everything okay? Is something bothering you?"

WHY MAKING FRIENDS IS IMPORTANT

Friendship is a beautiful part of life; if you have friends, you are lucky. Making friends is important for the following reasons:

There is a feeling of security that comes with having friends. There's something comforting about knowing that there's someone who truly knows and understands you, who watches out for you, and who you can depend on.

Making friends also provides an avenue for easy companionship. You have someone (or a set of people) to confide in about your feelings and to help you solve your problems.

Making friends also helps with self-esteem. Friendship brings a good sense of self-worth. Your friends make you feel loved and important.

WHO IS A GOOD FRIEND?

As important as it is to make friends, you don't want to run into the wrong crowds. You want good friends who will help you be a better person. Therefore, it's vital to know who a good friend is.

Let's look at some qualities that make a person a good friend.

#1 Trustworthiness

Trust is one of the biggest foundations of true friendship. Everyone wants a friend who they can trust.

A good friend is someone you can rely on and with whom you can share your secrets and burdens without any fear that they'll expose them to others.

Trust is a quality that shows you can always depend on someone to have your back, no matter what happens.

However, you don't have to be going through a bad time to know that a friend is trustworthy. The fact that you feel safe and secure around them is enough.

#2 Honesty

A good friend is someone who tells you the truth at all times. They won't lie to you or about you. Because they have your best interests at heart, they'll always tell you the truth, even when you don't like it.

However, a good friend will also try to say the truth nicely and in a way that doesn't hurt your feelings.

#3 Presence

A good friend is present. They'll often show up when you need them. Even when they're physically far away, they find a way to show their presence in your life. In essence, they keep in touch.

A good friend will actually be there when you need a listening ear or help. Of course, they won't just talk. But by their actions and presence in your life, you'll know they care about you.

#4 Kindness

A good friend will show their love for you by being kind to you. They're not mean or hurtful.

When you need help, they won't hesitate to provide it in the best way they can. They also don't keep the good things that they have to themselves. They'll like to share things with you, so you both can have the same good experience.

#5 Nonjudgmental

A good friend isn't critical or belittling. Instead, they love and accept you for who you are while helping you and cheering you on to become a better person.

Good friends will encourage you and help you get rid of any insecurity that you might have. They understand your struggles and experiences and help you get through them.

What's more, a good friend will respect your choices and decisions. They accept that you may not like the same things or agree on everything. Thus, they respect your differences.

#6 Loyalty

A good friend is loyal to you. When you do something wrong or make mistakes, a good friend finds it easy to forgive and stay with you. They remain on your side, in good and bad times, even when other people don't want to be around you.

Another sign of loyalty is that your friend will stand up for you when you're weak or absent. They won't allow others to put you down or bully you. Instead, they make excuses for you and won't believe anything they hear about you without first hearing your side of the story.

ARE YOU A GOOD FRIEND?

This is really an essential question to ask yourself, as you begin to exhibit friendship skills. The goal is not just to be a friend but to be a good friend who others can rely on and cherish.

We've already discussed and explained the qualities of a good friend.

So, the first question to ask yourself is, do you think you have all of these qualities? Or are there areas you need to work on to be a better friend?

You see, friendship is more than just playing with and enjoying the company of another person. It's beyond feeling good when you're around someone. It's also about loyalty, trust, and respect.

To be a good friend, you must spend quality time with your friend. Your shared experiences bring you and your friends closer, strengthening your friendship bond.

As a good friend, you should also be able to open up to your friends and let them into your private space. Friendship is a give-and-take. If you want your friends to always trust you, you must also show that you trust them.

Additionally, when your friend returns the gesture by opening up to you, you must never take them for granted. You should listen, support them, and always try to do what's best for them.

This is how you show that you sincerely care for them. The things you do will say more than words could ever express.

Also, good friends pay attention to each other's likes and dislikes. They're sensitive to their friends' emotions and can tell when their friends are uncomfortable with something. They understand that in a friendship, the little things matter.

Furthermore, good friends want the best for their friends. As such, they're willing to push and challenge one another to do better and be better.

In addition, being a good friend doesn't mean ignoring your friend's faults or wrongdoings. You should care too much to allow your friend to get away with doing what's wrong. Instead, you correct them firmly but with love.

Finally, you're not a good friend if you allow others to say bad things about your friends. Instead, you should show your loyalty by defending them.

Now that you know these things, can you really say that you are a good friend? Regardless of your answer, know that you can always improve your friendship skills.

FEELING LIKE AN OUTCAST?

Friendship groups give you a sense of community and belonging that can make you feel safe. However, sometimes people feel like they don't quite fit in anywhere. They feel like they are outside the social groups. Sometimes people call this feeling like an outcast, because they have been "cast out" of the group.

I can reliably assure you that you're not alone. Many of us have, at one point or the other, felt like outcasts.

Luckily, that feeling is usually temporary at certain moments of our life. Just because we feel that way sometimes doesn't mean we are destined to feel that way all the time. Everyone is capable of building friendships.

If you look closely enough, there's someone around who shares the same passions and interests as you. You only need to make them your friend. Fortunately, we've already discussed how to make friends. Now's the time to put that skill to the test!

Also, if you want to get into a group, you're likely to succeed if you focus on being friends with individual members of the group. It'll be much easier to get in the group that way.

Just note and pick out three members of the group you like the most. You might want to choose the ones that like the same things you do. Having something in common can help you start a conversation.

Interact and make friends with those three. Once those three people start to accept and respect you, you'll feel like less of an outcast with the rest of the group.

Another way to overcome this feeling is by using social media.

Using Social Media Positively

Many people use social media to stay connected to their friends. Platforms like Facebook, Instagram, and WhatsApp give people the opportunity to keep in touch with friends and share updates about what's going on in their lives.

What's more, these platforms give an opportunity for you to meet new people and make new friends.

However, many things can go wrong when using social media, so you need to learn how to use it positively and safely.

For one, you should set a fixed time limit for social media use. This is to make sure that you don't become addicted to social media or get distracted from doing other important things like schoolwork and house chores.

Having fixed times for social media will also help you focus on making friends with the people around you as well, not just focusing on virtual friends. Your parents will probably be the ones to set these limits for you, and they are correct in doing so.

You can also use social media to find people with similar interests. You can join online groups that have other kids your age who like the things you do or engage in the same activities.

For instance, if you like baking you can join an online baking platform and connect with people who share your passion. You'll enjoy discussing your interests and exchanging ideas and experiences.

Still, be careful when using social media. Don't try to keep up with everyone you meet on social media. Avoid people who ask for money or bully others online.

Also, don't focus on the acceptance of others. The need to be accepted by everyone will stop you from seeing how special you really are. Only stay friends with those who like you in return, and ensure that your parents know and approve of them.

KEEPING FRIENDS

The goal of developing friendship skills doesn't end with making friends. You need to learn to keep them as well.

Some of the best friendships are those that have lasted for decades — spanning through school, college, and beyond. It takes a lot of sacrifice to make a friendship last for that long. How can you achieve it?

Well, frequent communication is one way to ensure that your friendship keeps going. Even in situations where your friend lives in a different city, you can still interact online regularly. You should be able to give updates on each other's lives and try to visit physically at least once a year.

What You Can Do When a Friend Is in Trouble

You should always be there for your friends in times of trouble. Whenever a friend is going through a tough time, find ways to comfort them and show that you're there for them.

There are different ways you can do this. For instance, you can help a sick friend catch up with assignments and notes that they missed in class.

The goal is to always be present to make them feel loved and cherished.

Dealing with Misunderstandings

Friendly conflicts are a part of every friendship journey. A very important friendship skill to learn is how to deal with disagreements and misunderstandings productively and without leaving any lasting resentment or mistrust.

First, you must learn to talk things through. Don't be quick to believe what you hear about your friend without confirming the truth with them.

Ignoring your friends or giving them the silent treatment when you're upset about something they did or said isn't the best way to resolve conflicts. Instead, bring up the issue with your friend, talk about it, and resolve the matter quickly. The longer the issue drags on, the harder it is to truly fix.

When resolving issues, you must know the correct time and place to bring up certain matters. Try to avoid public arguments with your friend. It's always better to resolve issues in private to avoid embarrassing scenes.

Most importantly, learn to say sorry and be quick to forgive faults. No one is perfect and everyone, including you, has flaws. So you'll need to learn to endure some things you may not like, as long as they aren't hurtful to anyone.

Differences are normal. What if someone doesn't like the same things that you like? Can you still be friends with them? There are some differences that you can live with. If you choose to remain friends with the person, you must learn to embrace that difference. With time, as you support each other, your differences can be something that forge the friendship bond and make it even stronger. And you can support and cheer each other on to achieve your different dreams.

ACTIVITIES

Here are some activities that you can do to develop your friendship skills:

#1 Try interacting with the other kids in school during breaks or events. In your journal, note down the friendship skills you think you struggle with. Think of ways that you can practice developing those skills. Also, note the improvements you make. With practice, it can only get better.

#2 If you have struggled to make friends or meet new people, you can:

> Practice introducing yourself in front of the mirror every day before you go to school.

Have a friendship challenge. Plan to introduce yourself to at least five new people every week.

At the end of each week, write down the names of the new people you introduced yourself to, especially the ones who were nicest to you, and then...

Say hi to them the following week and try to hold a conversation. The purpose of the conversation should be to discover the people who share something in common with you. This should help you streamline your friendship options.

#3 Join a group consisting of people who enjoy something you love. For instance, you can combine a dance class if you love dancing or an online science club if you are passionate about anything scientific.

CHAPTER FIVE:

COOPERATION SKILLS

Building tree houses and creating science projects are examples of activities that are more fun with a partner or two. The work gets done better and faster, even if there may be one or two quarrels in the mix. It's part of the process. What is it that helps you and your partner complete that task? It's called cooperation.

Cooperation is when two or more people work together toward a shared goal. When you work with others to do something, you cooperate. However, to cooperate you have to agree, and each person has to do their part.

People cooperate with others in many things. As a kid, you will use cooperative skills at school, for projects, at play, at home, with siblings, and so on. It's hard to avoid it. You always need people for one thing or the other, so knowing how to cooperate is very important.

If you didn't know how to cooperate before now, don't sweat it. This chapter will help you do just that. We'll go over what cooperation is about and how you can build cooperative skills. In the end, you'll be the real team player everyone wants to work with.

WHAT IS COOPERATION?

Cooperation is working with others to get something done. It can be doing a chore, organizing a surprise party, finishing an art project, acting out a school play, or just about anything else that is a shared goal.

Cooperation also applies when you work with your parents to do what they tell you to do. When you don't, you're not cooperating with them, and this can be a very sticky situation because no one is pleased and things don't get done well or on time.

Sometimes when you're cooperating, you may not have to do anything but just be on a particular side or team. For example, cooperating to throw a surprise party for your dad may only require you to not spill the beans about it to your dad. That would ruin the surprise!

The beauty of cooperating is seeing what you've achieved with others. It's usually better to work with others than to be alone in a lot of things. You know what they usually say: "Two heads are better than one."

To have cooperation skills means you should be:

#1 A Good Listener:

Thankfully, we've covered listening skills in Chapter 3. When cooperating with others, you need to listen to them, and they need to listen to you.

Everyone shares their thoughts or ideas about the work to be done, and when there is no active listening, you will miss out on what is said. This can have a terrible effect on the work or project.

Listening to others doesn't mean you have to totally agree with them. In fact, you may disagree entirely, but you'll only know this if you listen carefully. In the end, everyone can come to a compromise after hearing what each person has to say. This helps with the planning. So in every team you are in, listen actively to what everyone has to say.

#2 Clear Communication:

To cooperate with others successfully, there has to be clear communication within the group. This includes information on when to meet, what to do, how to do it, who is sick or absent, and so on. These details have to be clearly communicated.

#3 Own Up to Mistakes:

Don't pass on the blame when you're wrong. Making mistakes or errors doesn't make you a bad person or less smart; everyone makes mistakes sometimes.

So, when you're working with others and you make a mistake, own up to it. Keeping quiet about a mistake can affect the whole project. It's best to let your teammates know so you can work together to figure out the best way forward.

Sometimes the mistake can be fixed quickly; sometimes, it's not even a big deal. Owning up to your mistakes actually shows that you're responsible and mature, and people will likely trust you more.

#4 Respect Others:

This is super important in cooperation skills. You can't interrupt others when they are speaking. You should respect their ideas and if you don't really agree with them, respectfully say so. You can say something like, "Wow Alice, that's a nice idea but what if we do this instead, what do you think?"

When you say it like this, you're more likely to get others to like your idea without hurting the other person.

#5 Recognize Your Strengths and Weaknesses and Those of Your Teammates:

Find out what you're good at and what you fail at. Often, your friends or teammates make up for your weaknesses, and your strengths make up for theirs.

This is what makes working with others amazing. You receive support and can offer others support as well. In the end, everyone takes the credit for a job well done.

As great as cooperation is, remember that working with others can have some problems. But you can handle these with the right attitude.

Forgive quickly, don't get easily upset, focus on the job, care about others' feelings, and help however you can. We bet you and your teammates will do just fine with these skills in mind.

WHY ARE COOPERATION SKILLS IMPORTANT?

From all you've learned so far, you can see that cooperation skills are important. However, just in case, here are more reasons why cooperation skills are important:

- With cooperation, you can get things done faster and better.
- Cooperation skills make you a better teammate and others will like to work with you.

- People trust and rely on you more when you cooperate easily.
- You form better friendships and bonds.
- You learn more when you're able to cooperate with others.
- Others have your back and support you when you cooperate with them.
- Cooperation skills help with communication.
- With cooperation skills, you will receive help when you need it and give service where you can.

HAVING A GOOD SENSE OF HUMOR

You may have heard someone say, "She has such a good sense of humor!" Maybe you've wondered what that really means.

Well, humor is interesting in a funny way. Comedy, jokes, and silly movies are all forms of humor. When we say a person has a good sense of humor, it usually means they laugh easily or are good at making others laugh. Telling jokes might come easily to them, and they're good at finding the silly side of any situation and helping others to enjoy it as well.

We aren't all meant to be comedians and you might not feel like you're the funniest person in your family or social group. That's okay! You can still develop and enjoy your own sense of humor.

You know you have a good sense of humor when:

- You love to laugh. Laughter is actually very good for you!
- You enjoy finding things that are silly in any situation.
- You like trying to make your friends laugh through making funny comments or doing funny behaviors.

- You enjoy watching humorous television or movies, or reading silly books.

People like being around others who are able to laugh at jokes or silly situations. People also feel good about themselves when they can make someone else laugh.

Other ways of expressing your sense of humor could be that you:

Don't sulk when you make mistakes, but rather, laugh at them. Mistakes show our weaknesses, and sometimes we are tempted to think, "I'm just not good enough." This shouldn't be so. If you have a good sense of humor, you should be able to move on from your mistakes and even laugh about them.

Have a creative mind and imagination. Good-humored people know how to come up with quick jokes and to find something that is funny or fun in any situation.

Are kind. It's one thing to tell a joke and another to tell a mean joke. No one likes being the target of an unkind joke. A good sense of humor means you don't need to hurt someone's feelings to say a joke. Always remember that it's not clever to be mean.

Make people laugh easily. Maybe you're good at remembering jokes you heard on TV or read in a book, or maybe you're good at making up your own jokes. Either way, it can feel really good to make other people laugh when you're trying to be funny.

Have a positive attitude. Even when bad things happen to you, you know there's no use crying over spilled milk. Making the best of a situation and focusing on the positive can be good for your sense of humor.

BENEFITS OF A HAVING
A GOOD SENSE OF HUMOR

What does a good sense of humor have to do with cooperation or anything? Plenty. For one, doing hard work—for example, on a project—can make people feel tense. Laughter lightens the mood and helps people think better.

Another benefit of having a good sense of humor is that it makes you more approachable. This means that others see you as friendly, nice, and easy to talk to.

Humor helps you relax. Those with a good sense of humor may have the ability to think and work better. You may have heard that laughter is the best medicine—this is often true! Spending some time focused on things that make you laugh can make a lot of our problems feel smaller.

With a good sense of humor, you may find that you're a bit tougher or less likely to have your feelings hurt. If you can always see the silly side of a situation, then you won't take what others say and do so seriously. This may help you to protect your feelings when others are unkind.

Having a good sense of humor means you're creative, and your mind is quite sharp. This means you can come up with solutions to problems quickly and in a creative way.

People like to listen to someone with a good sense of humor. So it's easy to get your teammates, classmates, and siblings to listen to you.

Humor helps you with communicating and sharing your ideas. People find it easier to accept your thoughts when you express them in a humorous way.

When a person with a good sense of humor is around, an ugly situation can quickly turn into a happy one.

There are so many more benefits that come from having a good sense of humor. So get your funny bone moving and find out.

LEARNING TO EASE TENSION WITH HUMOR

Tension can build up and bother us at times. Sometimes it's because of a test, a project, or even planning a trip. It can be quite tiring to be under all that tension. So how can you relieve yourself of this?

- Have friends who know how to share a joke.
- Read funny books.
- Watch funny movies.
- Think up a funny story or scene and maybe even act it out.
- Laugh at others' jokes.
- Don't beat yourself up when you make a mistake. There's almost always something funny even in a bad situation.

DIFFERENTIATING BETWEEN LAUGHING WITH AND LAUGHING AT

When you laugh *with* someone, it means you both found the joke funny and you are enjoying it together. When you laugh *at* someone, it means that person is the target of the joke, he or she didn't find it funny, and what you are doing is unkind.

Laughing at someone isn't a nice thing to do. You should not get your comedy at someone else's expense. It's rude and insensitive to do, and you'll end up hurting someone else's feelings.

Sometimes someone may make a mistake, and you laugh at them, expecting them to laugh with you. But if you see that they aren't laughing, stop laughing and apologize. You can also make the situation better by sharing a similar thing that happened to you. That way, the person may forget their bad situation and laugh with you.

If you don't like to be the butt of a joke, don't create that situation for others.

TREATING OTHERS WITH KINDNESS, RESPECT, AND PATIENCE

We bet you like it when others are kind to you, respect you, and are patient with you. Well, they'll also like it if you do the same to them. Just how should you go about it?

- Learn to say sorry, please, and thank you.
- Listen when others are speaking. Don't be quick to disagree with their ideas.
- Look at people when you're talking to them; don't look away.
- Compliment others' good work and don't take credit for it.
- Show that you care when something bad happens to someone else.
- Share what you have.
- If you disagree with someone else, do it nicely.
- Help when you're needed.

- Be friendly and easy to talk to.
- Don't laugh when someone makes a mistake or hurt their feelings by making a bad joke.
- Don't shout at someone when you want them to do something for you or when they make a mistake.

In all, remember the golden rule: treat others as you want them to treat you. So think, "What would I want to be done for me in this situation?" Do the same for others.

ACTIVITIES

Do you think you know enough about cooperation? Let's put it to the test with these activities.

- Work together to create an artistic masterpiece.
- Cook with your friends.
- Do chemistry together.
- Work on a science project.
- Solve a jigsaw puzzle.
- Compete as a team in a math quiz.
- Put on a play.
- Run a relay race.
- Play soccer in teams.

These fun activities will put your cooperation skills to the test. You'll get to see how well you work with others and how well you handle criticism.

Go, team!

CHAPTER SIX:

NEGOTIATION & PROBLEM-SOLVING SKILLS

There are times when what you want is different from what other people want. One example might be when you wish to stay up past your bedtime for a special event, and your parents insist that you go to bed at the usual time.

The conflicting desires create a problem. Given the situation at hand, solving this problem might require using negotiation.

Negotiation is a very important social skill that can be used in the most basic situations—like the one described above—as well as the most important—such as major negotiations that occur between countries to determine international treaties.

The act of negotiation is important for everyone to practice and become comfortable with, as it's essential in our attempts to compromise, seek fair outcomes, and get along with others.

This chapter will help you understand what negotiation is all about and how you can use it as a social and problem-solving skill.

WHAT IS NEGOTIATION?

Negotiation refers to the dialogue that takes place between two or more people trying to reach an acceptable agreement.

During a negotiation, each of the parties (also known as negotiators) attempts to persuade the others to accept their point of view, or at least to develop a compromise that reflects the interests of everyone involved. To use the example above, your parents might agree on a slightly later bedtime that still accomplishes their goal for you to get enough sleep, with your goal to participate in at least part of the event. You would work toward that compromise through the act of negotiation.

Don't think of a negotiation as being similar to an argument. In an argument, typically the goal is for someone to win (e.g., to be right, or to get what they want). In contrast, in a negotiation, everyone wins by getting at least some of what they want.

WHY ARE NEGOTIATION SKILLS IMPORTANT?

There are many reasons why negotiation skills are important. Here are the benefits of negotiation skills:

#1 Confidence

Negotiation skills give you the confidence to explain to other people exactly what you want and why. Negotiation allows you to express your own opinion instead of just agreeing to what everyone else says even when you're unhappy about it.

#2 Ability to Resolve Conflicts

It's natural for you to experience conflicting interests with your parents, siblings, or friends from time to time. But with negotiation skills, it becomes easier to resolve those conflicts when they arise.

#3 Becoming a Better Listener

One of the important advantages of negotiation skills is that they make you a better listener. Many people lack the ability to listen with rapt attention to the views of others, and this can really make it hard for them to find common ground. Negotiation requires you to listen carefully to the other person's perspective so that you can develop a reasonable compromise. It's a great opportunity to practice those active listening skills.

#4 Increase in Empathy

Negotiation skills help to develop your sense of empathy. Empathy simply means being able to understand and share the feelings of another individual. We will discuss empathy at greater length later in this book.

#5 Better Relationships

Great relationships are built on the ability to resolve disagreements whenever they arise. Negotiation skills give you the ability to resolve disagreements with others, allowing you to have better and long-lasting relationships with the people around you.

#6 Increase Communication Skills

Constant negotiations with other people provide you with the opportunity to improve your communication skills. Consequently, this allows you to learn how you can craft your words most compellingly.

WHAT IS PROBLEM-SOLVING?

Problem-solving is the process of developing a solution that helps to overcome an obstacle that stands in the way of your goal or what you need to do.

For example, you might need to problem-solve if the shirt you need to wear to soccer practice is still in the laundry when you need it. What could be a solution for that problem?

Or you might get to school and then realize that you forgot your lunch at home. How would you solve that problem?

There are many possible solutions to each of the problems described above. When we are solving a problem, we're often faced with several possible solutions. Our task is to think through which solution will get us to our goal the most effectively and without creating any new problems along the way.

In this book, we are focused on social skills, so we're going to be learning about problem-solving specifically as a social skill, which means the ways we solve problems that occur between people. One example is the one we already discussed, when you and your parents have different ideas about bedtime. Some other examples of problems between people might be:

> You are working as part of a group of four on an art project, but one person never shows up to help with the project. So now, your group is behind schedule and you don't know what to do about the person who isn't helping.

You want to go shopping with a friend on Saturday at 2pm, and you need your dad to drive you. But your brother has been asking your dad to teach him how to ride his bike, and they agreed to do it on Saturday afternoon. There's no way for your dad to do what both you and your brother want at the same time.

These are both problems between people and you'll need strong social skills to solve them.

There are several steps that make up the act of problem-solving. These steps are:

#1 Identifying the Problem

Identifying or finding the problem is the first step in problem-solving. We can only solve problems that we're able to clearly identify. That's the reason why it is important to first point out the problem you are facing.

#2 Finding Out the Reason for the Problem

This step has to do with finding out the cause of the problem. Where is this problem coming from? Is there one specific thing that's causing this problem? When you know the cause of a problem, you will be able to come up with precise solutions that address that cause.

#3 Developing Possible Solutions

Once you have identified the root cause of the problem, the next line of action is to create several possible solutions. Doing this will allow you to have different options you can choose from. For

example, for the group project, some of the options could be –
work hard as a group of three to finish the project without the
fourth person, or talk to the kid who isn't participating and ask
them to help more, or yell at the kid who isn't helping and accuse
them of being lazy, or tell the teacher that the fourth kid isn't
helping and is a bad teammate, or ask your teacher for an
extension on the deadline for the project.

#4 Choosing the Best Solution and Applying It

Choosing the best solution demands that you consider each of the
possible solutions properly to determine which is best.
Remember, you want to choose a solution that (a) solves the
problem and also (b) does not create any new problems. In the
above example, if you decide to yell at the kid who isn't helping
and accuse them of being lazy, that could lead to hurt feelings and
even more trouble. Rather than solving your problem, it gave you
new problems! So choose the solution that will have the fewest
negative side effects. After selecting the best option, you'll go
ahead and act on that solution.

#5 Evaluating the Result

After you try the solution you chose, you'll find out whether or
not it worked, or whether its effects were positive or negative. In
a situation where the result is not what you wanted, or where new
problems emerge, you'll have to start the problem-solving process
again.

WHY ARE PROBLEM-SOLVING SKILLS IMPORTANT?

There are so many advantages that problem-solving skills have to offer. These advantages will help you both in the present and future, in social situations and in other areas of your life. They include:

Identification of Problems

Problem-solving skills give you the ability to identify exactly what the problem is. This is important when trying to come up with the right solution.

Brainstorming

Problem-solving skills allow you to brainstorm your way out of difficult situations. Brainstorming is essential when playing games, performing extracurricular activities, or working on any academic activity. It's also important in carrying out daily activities and working with a team.

Great Academic Results

When you have acquired problem-solving skills, it will be easier for you to perform better in academic activities. This is because problem-solving skills enhance your analytical skills, consequently allowing you to have a deeper understanding of the lessons taught.

Increased Confidence

Being able to regularly solve problems whenever they arise is a way of increasing your confidence. You may find that you're less afraid of trying out something new and tackling new challenges.

WHEN TO NEGOTIATE OR COMPROMISE

Negotiation or a compromise should take place when the opinion or desire of another person does not align with yours.

For instance, if you and your sibling share a single bicycle, it would be appropriate to negotiate or reach a compromise if there is an argument over whose turn it is to ride the bike for the day.

In such a situation, you and your sibling can decide to take turns riding the bicycle for a set time that day.

YOU CAN'T ALWAYS HAVE YOUR OWN WAY

While it's true that negotiation allows you to reach an acceptable settlement, you should understand that you can't always have your own way, no matter how great a negotiator you may be. There are times when negotiation fails to produce the result you want.

This can happen to anybody, even to an experienced negotiator. When this happens, you must learn to accept whatever the result might be and move on.

For instance, if you were unable to persuade your parents to let you do your chores another day, you will need to go ahead and follow their instructions. However, you can ask your parents for the reason why they don't want you to postpone the chores for later so that at least you understand the thinking behind their decision.

KNOWING THOSE THINGS THAT AREN'T NEGOTIABLE

Some things are nonnegotiable, whether with your parents or anyone who is in charge of your well-being and activities. Here are some of those things:

Safety

It would be impossible to negotiate your safety with someone who has the responsibility of taking care of you. For instance, you can't persuade your parents to allow you to ride your bike down the street in the dark if you live on a busy street and doing so would be dangerous.

Good Behavior/Manners

Good behavior is not negotiable. Good behaviors involve greeting anyone who arrives, using respectful language, and saying thank you whenever someone assists you in any way. It also includes using the words like "please" and "may I" when need be.

Good Hygiene

Good hygiene should be maintained and kept at all times and cannot be negotiated. You should ensure that you clean your room, shower or bathe regularly, brush your teeth, trim your nails, and generally take care of your body and your space.

PRACTICE NEGOTIATING

Regularly practicing your negotiation skills can make you more confident and more effective when it's time to use them. Being good at negotiating means having a high success rate in resolving conflicts or disagreements.

If you fail to practice your negotiating skills for a period of time, your skills will begin to decline, just like any other skill you stop practicing. To avoid this, you can frequently practice negotiating with those around you, such as your parents, siblings, teachers, and your friends.

Also, it's important to note that it's not enough to only read about negotiation skills. You should always make sure to put whatever you have read into practice.

LEARNING TO SEE DIFFERENT VIEWPOINTS

Being able to learn or see from other people's perspectives is a skill that can help you when negotiating or trying to solve a problem.

When you can see things from other people's points of view, you'll be able to come up with solutions that are more likely to please everyone involved in a negotiation.

Here are some ways you can learn to see things from different viewpoints:

Listen Attentively to Other People

Listening attentively to people with opposing perspectives can help you to see things from their point of view. It's important to note that you are listening to understand and not for the sole purpose of forming a response.

Ask Questions

Asking questions is one of the ways to understand other people's perspectives. However, you should ask questions because you are genuinely trying to understand and not because you are trying to ridicule their point of view. In other words, make sure your questions are polite and sincere.

Do Research

If you want to see things from other people's perspectives, you should try to learn what you can about their perspectives. This might mean reading a variety of books or magazines that reflect different viewpoints.

IT'S OKAY TO CHANGE YOUR OPINION

It's natural to have a change of opinion from time to time. As a matter of fact, changing your mind about things is proof that you are an open-minded person who is ready to analyze and question the opinions you hold. This is a good thing! In most cases, a change of opinion takes place after you have been exposed to new information.

BEING OPEN TO NEW THINGS

You can't be a great negotiator or problem solver if you are not open to new things. Being open to new things means that you are receptive to new information, experiences, and/or ideas. There are several benefits that come from being open to new ideas and information.

For one, it helps you to gain more knowledge and to think critically and rationally. Also, being open-minded increases your sense of empathy, as you will be willing to listen to other people's views even when they are totally different from yours.

Furthermore, this ability allows you to have more than one approach to solving a problem. For instance, when doing a math assignment, your friend might know of one method of answering a question, and you might have another. If you are open to your friend's strategy, you might gain some new skills along the way. Ultimately, you'll know multiple ways of answering the math question instead of just one.

ACTIVITIES

Here are a few fun activities to help you develop your negotiation and problem-solving skills:

- Play the game of Monopoly with your friends and family. Monopoly is a board game that encourages the use of negotiation or problem-solving skills.
- The next time you want to request something from someone, prepare counter offers just in case they decline your initial offer.
- Watch shows where you can find people negotiating among themselves and try to practice what you have watched with your family or friends.

CHAPTER SEVEN:

RESPONSIBILITY SKILLS

When you think of the word "responsibility," what's the first thing that comes to mind? Work? Duty? Do you dodge it like you would a dodge ball?

Well, you can stop doing that now. Responsibility isn't as scary as you think.

You can be what the adults call "responsible" if you know how to go about it.

With responsibility skills, you can handle whatever task or duty is given to you, and do so effectively.

In this chapter, you'll learn what responsibility is, why it's important, and how you can sharpen your responsibility skills.

WHAT IS RESPONSIBILITY?

Responsibility means having a duty to carry out or being in control over people, events, or things. So we say a person is going to be held responsible for something when they have to answer for the duty they were given.

If you're a responsible person, it means you are mindful of your duties and where others are relying on you, and you ensure that others can depend on you. You also make decisions they can trust and make contributions they will value.

For instance, a duty could be to watch your younger siblings or to care for the class pet. You don't want to return with a sick pet because you forgot to feed it, or worse, let your little brother drink from the toilet!

There are usually consequences for not carrying out a duty or responsibility. For one, you may be considered irresponsible and untrustworthy.

WHY ARE RESPONSIBILITY SKILLS IMPORTANT?

Responsibility skills are essential in everyday life. If you have these skills, you'll easily stand out. They show up in being dependable, making good choices, ensuring that things are done correctly, and owning up to your mistakes.

Some of the things that responsibility skills will help you with include:

Purpose

Responsibility gives you a purpose. You feel like someone trusts you to get something done, and for that period of time, you feel like you have a purpose to carry out.

Having a purpose is important as it gives you something to look forward to. Also, a level of confidence comes with achieving each task.

Punctuality

Responsibility skills teach you how to manage your time wisely. You learn to do things when you're supposed to, which helps you achieve more and be more hardworking.

Organization

With responsibility skills, you'll be able to get more organized. It helps to figure out the things you have to do and break each task down into easy steps. Then you can enjoy crossing each step off your to-do list.

Leadership

Leaders have to be responsible. So, when you learn how to take responsibility and handle it properly, don't be surprised when you start to get many leadership roles.

Boosts Self Esteem

Being responsible gives you a feeling of being capable and this, in turn, boosts your self-esteem. You'll feel good knowing you've done well and others are pleased with you.

Builds Trust

People trust those who are responsible because they know that whatever is given to them is in good hands. They also know they can depend and rely on you, which is very important.

BALANCING RESPONSIBILITIES AND DESIRES

More often than not, we don't feel like doing what we're supposed to do. Even worse, we sometimes feel like doing stuff we're not supposed to do.

As such, our responsibilities and desires may often be in conflict. Here's an example.

Your parents instructed you to watch your siblings while they go out for a dinner date. However, that's the same night as a concert by your favorite band. You know the effort and time it took you and your friends to get those tickets.

What will you do? Will you ditch this responsibility and give in to your desire to go to the concert? Or will you forget about the show and do as you've been told?

This is where responsibility skills help. You need to find that balance between fulfilling your responsibilities and giving in to your desires.

You must first realize that responsibility comes first every time. While this may seem hard and boring, you'll be glad that you chose the higher road later.

However, being responsible doesn't mean that you'll never get to do what you want. It just means understanding that there's a time for everything and everything has its proper place.

For instance, rather than spending your entire afternoon on Tiktok, you can take time to do your homework. Tiktok will still be there when you're done with your homework.

Most people fail at learning responsibility because they can't balance the time for their desires and the time for duty.

One of the ways you can balance desire and responsibility is by having set times for specific tasks and following them accordingly. For example, when you get home from school, you can do your homework, take out the trash, and do your other chores before spending time playing video games.

Also, plan specific times for the leisure activities you enjoy so that you won't spend too much time on them and consequently fail at your responsibilities.

BECOMING INDEPENDENT

As you take more responsibility for yourself, you'll notice that you grow more independent. This is because you will have spent time growing and learning to manage certain situations on your own. As such, you'll be more confident and better prepared when the time comes to step out on your own.

Your responsibility skills will pay off in these situations:

When You Need a Job

Responsibility is one of the top attributes that employers seek when they are hiring. Being able to show that you have a history of responsible behavior and staying on top of what you're supposed to do will be beneficial to you when you're applying for jobs. You can then use your organizing, planning, and time management skills when working and become a great member of the team.

With Your Money

Responsibility skills will help you manage your money better. Building responsibility will enable you to budget and not splurge on things you don't need.

When you're responsible with your money, you're more likely to always have enough for what you need. As you grow older, you'll be glad you learned to use your money responsibly.

ACTIVITIES

Below are a number of things you can do to practice the lessons you've learned about responsibility.

Create a Schedule for Your Entire Week

Sit with your parents and draw up a plan for your week. If that's too challenging, create a schedule for the next two days and ask your parents to help remind you to follow this plan.

Remember that the goal is to be able to manage your time, be organized, and carry out your duties. Be sure to include your chores on your schedule—add time for things like feeding your pet or emptying the dishwasher.

While it may seem difficult at first, you'll soon see the benefits of having all your duties listed out and doing them when you should.

Keep Your Personal Space Organized

Try to maintain a clean and organized space around you, including your bedroom and your locker or desk at school.

Help the Adults Around You with Chores

You can decide to take on a specific chore that you'll be responsible for, like mowing the yard, doing the dishes, or babysitting. Any time you leave these tasks undone, you could put a quarter in a jar as a consequence of neglecting your responsibility.

Get a Job

Sure, you're just a kid, but who said there were no jobs for children?

You can ask your parents or teachers to give you a task for which you'll be responsible. You can also volunteer in an area you're interested in. For instance, if you like animals, you might be able to volunteer at an animal rescue.

You can also ask for odd jobs from your neighbors or family friends. You may be able to earn some cash by mowing their lawns or shoveling their driveways when it snows.

Having a job provides you a sense of responsibility as others begin to rely on you to complete specific tasks and do what is expected of you. It can also help you with time management.

CHAPTER EIGHT:

ENGAGEMENT AND ATTENTION SKILLS

This chapter talks about essential social skills including engagement and attention. These skills are important because if you practice and become good at them, they can help you to approach other skills more effectively.

Before we go on, let's talk about what engagement means and what engagement skills are.

WHAT IS ENGAGEMENT?

Engagement means becoming involved with somebody or something in an attempt to understand them. It includes the ability to hold another person's attention while interacting socially with them.

When we meet and interact with others, it's usually not for no reason at all. We usually have a desire to know, understand, and/or learn from the people with whom we interact. Understanding this will allow you to interact with others more effectively.

Engagement is more than just having a conversation. It also includes the active ability to perceive and understand other people, while keeping their attention as well. It involves attempting to connect with others, paying attention to others, and thinking about their opinions.

When you learn to engage with others, it will help you and those you engage with feel confident because they will know that their opinions matter.

WHY ARE ENGAGEMENT SKILLS IMPORTANT?

Engagement skills guide you through various parts of life. When you engage with someone, you start to determine the kind of person they are, perhaps learning new things about people that you may not have known before. This information gives you a better guide on how to approach and relate to them.

Other reasons why building engagement skills is important include the following:

#1 Boosting Your Confidence.

When you are able to engage with others effectively — tuning in to their thoughts and feelings, while also communicating your interest to them and keeping their attention — you may find that you begin to feel more confident. This is because engaging with others can lead to gratifying social connections. As social creatures, humans need these types of connections, and when we have them frequently, we can feel more confident and happier.

The more you practice engaging with others and keeping others engaged with you, the better you will get at it. Through this process, you may learn a lot of new things from the people you're engaging with, and with this new knowledge will come new confidence.

#2 Improving Your Communication Ability

Engagement skills help you find better ways to communicate. Being engaged, and keeping others engaged with you, requires using effective and adaptable communication that is appropriate to the particular person and situation. As you get better at adapting your communication over time, your abilities as a communicator will grow stronger.

Failures of communication can be very frustrating, and some thoughts and feelings are hard to explain to others. Many people give up in these situations and keep those thoughts and feelings to themselves, but that often doesn't feel very good and may not be the most productive approach. Instead, by developing stronger, more adaptable communication, you may start to find it easier to express even your complicated thoughts and feelings.

#3 Improving Your Creativity and Critical Thinking

Engagement skills encourage your mind to be free, curious, and inquisitive. You have to be curious and inquisitive in order to learn about others, so these skills go hand in hand. As you spend more time being curious, you may find that your sense of creativity also begins to flourish.

With practice, you become an "expert" on how to relate to people and take on new tasks.

#4 Giving Introverts a Chance

83

An introvert is someone who likes to have plenty of time alone, rather than always being surrounded by others. In contrast, an extrovert typically likes to spend most of their time with other people and doesn't want or need a lot of alone time.

Engagement skills can help anyone interact with others more effectively, even if you are someone who generally prefers to be alone. Even the quietest or most shy person among us has a great deal to teach and share with others; by approaching interactions with a sense of curiosity, we are able to better appreciate what others have to offer.

LEARNING HOW TO MAKE OTHERS FEEL COMFORTABLE

Making others comfortable is an outcome of engagement skills. People feel good when they can tell that someone else is interested in them and is really listening to what they say; this tends to put people at ease.

You have to know what it feels like to be comfortable before you can make others feel comfortable. You should understand that being comfortable comes with peace, happiness, and a sense of belonging.

Below are a few things you can do to help others feel comfortable:

#1 Put on a Happy Face

A friendly smile is typically interpreted as being pleasant and approachable in the U.S. Greeting someone with a small smile can provide the listener with a sense of relaxation and give them room to express themselves in the best way.

Wearing a smile can also help you relax and collect your thoughts. This will help you communicate your thoughts and ideas more clearly.

#2 Compliment Others

There is a balance between compliments and flattery. Compliments are nice comments you make about someone or something—they are true and sincere. Flattery is excessive praise—it's usually insincere and is made with the aim of getting something in return.

When your parents, older siblings, or teachers compliment you, ask them to explain why they complimented you. This will help you know how and when to compliment others.

You need to understand that you don't have to compliment a person if it isn't true. You should also know that compliments should never come from a pressured heart. This will guide you to express yourself sincerely.

#3 Pay Close Attention

Even though it can be difficult, it's important to know how to intentionally listen to whoever is speaking to you.

Whatever is worth doing, no matter how small, is worth paying attention. When you carry out activities together, pay attention to others and learn to focus on tasks.

Pay attention to whoever you are interacting with. It will encourage the person to speak more, knowing that you are paying attention.

#4 Ask Polite Questions

Asking questions is how we learn about new things, and it's a very important part of life, especially during childhood. Hopefully you are already in the habit of asking questions to those around you whenever you don't quite understand what was said or what is happening.

When asking questions, be sure that the questions you're asking are polite and respectful. Sometimes, it's hard to know which questions are okay to ask and which are not. For example, it's fine to ask an adult what they do for their job, but most adults consider it rude when someone asks how much they get paid at their job. Another example is that it's fine to ask a kid how old they are, but many adults don't like to be asked that question.

Do your best to be polite and respectful, and if you accidentally ask a question that someone doesn't like, simply apologize and say you didn't realize it would be a rude question. That is an innocent mistake and over time you'll develop a better sense of which questions are great to ask and which should perhaps be avoided in certain situations.

IDENTIFYING EMBARRASSING MOMENTS FOR OTHERS

Embarrassing moments are moments when people feel ashamed, shy, or uncomfortable around others. It often comes with feeling out of place when something embarrassing happens.

Everyone gets embarrassed, but some more than others. Identifying other people's embarrassing moments will help you know how to deal with them.

Being able to identify other people's embarrassing moments is related to your engagement skills. Here are a few tips to help you know when someone around you is embarrassed:

- The person constantly avoids eye contact.
- The person stammers or stutters.
- The person is shy and not calm.
- The person is always apologizing for things they don't need to apologize for.

The above are some common ways that people who are embarrassed may act. But to know these things is not enough. Learning to handle them is what makes you skillful at communication and engagement.

Embarrassed people feel unsettled and would like to feel comfortable. Learning to help them feel comfortable will allow them relax and engage with you.

AVOIDING HOT TOPICS

Hot topics are controversial or inappropriate topics that come up in conversations. They may be trending or not, but it's helpful to know the hard topics to avoid when you get into conversations with others. Ask your parents to tell you about topics to avoid in conversations with others.

You don't have to have an opinion about everything.

There are some topics not to bring up when speaking to people in certain situations where you know those people might be particularly sensitive to a particular topic. For example, if you know a friend's pet has died recently, then you might want to avoid talking about your own pet for a while as a way to be sensitive to your friend's feelings. If you're not sure, it's fine to ask people whether they want to talk about something or not.

Sometimes you may be in a conversation that turns toward topics that make you uncomfortable, whatever those may be. If you're talking to adults or older children, you can politely but clearly explain that you would prefer not to have the conversation.

With kids your age, you can clearly or explicitly end the conversation and change the subject. Tell them why it's not appropriate to discuss the topic, especially if someone else brought it up.

The following tips are helpful:

#1 Excuse Yourself

If the topic is inappropriate, excuse yourself and leave immediately. You don't have to leave in a rash manner. Learn to simply say, "Excuse me, I have something I have to do."

#2 Change Topics

If you can take charge of the conversation, quickly change the topic to something else that everyone feels comfortable discussing. You can do this in a playful or respectful manner so it does not offend anyone.

#3 Say Nothing

You should understand that sometimes silence is the loudest way to speak. You can be quiet and listen without making any contributions. It may give the other person a clue to end the conversation.

#4 Be Compassionate

Learn how to put yourself in others' shoes. If you were that someone, would you feel comfortable discussing that topic? Learning to be compassionate will help you build a strong character. Compassion is an important tool to help others feel comfortable while you engage with them.

HELPING OTHERS THROUGH UNCOMFORTABLE SITUATIONS

Everyone can be of help to those around them, and kids are no exception. You can help others through uncomfortable situations in the most heartwarming ways. And with the right skills, you can learn to communicate your assistance or support even better.

Below are some ways you can do so:

#1 Give Encouraging Words

Encouraging words can go a long way to ease people's discomfort. Encouraging others will often make them feel better.

You can adopt common encouraging words into your vocabulary. Think of the times when words of encouragement have helped you through uncomfortable situations.

Learn to use sentences like, "You're going to do great." "It will be fine." "You did your best and you will do better next time." "I used to have the same experience too," etc. Practice when and how to use these sentences.

#2 A Hug for Friends

Give comforting hugs to people who are in uncomfortable situations, if you know them well and know that they are someone who appreciates hugs. It's a good idea to ask first if someone would like a hug. Then, hug them while saying words of encouragement to them.

#3 Provide Distraction

Sometimes we aren't able to solve problems for our friends, but providing them with a little bit of distraction can still be helpful. Offering to do something fun together, or telling your friend a joke, may lighten their mood at least for a little while and give them a break from whatever's bothering them.

DEALING WITH CONFLICTS

Conflict simply means disagreements among two or more people. Conflicts occur naturally among kids, and knowing how to deal with conflicts is an important skill to learn. Whether it's a conflict with siblings or other playmates, you don't have to avoid the person or people involved. Instead, make an effort to settle conflicts in the best way possible.

Here are some tips that can help you:

#1 Learn to Talk and Listen

"Talk" doesn't mean "Yell!" When you face a conflict, discuss it with the other person. You must learn to listen to the person's opinions and express yourself without screaming or throwing insults.

You can take a break to collect your emotions and think things through before going back to discussing them with the other person. That will give you a chance to also consider the other person's views.

#2 Know When to Involve an Older Person

When you can't settle your conflict with other kids, speak to an older person (preferably a parent or a teacher). The adult can then help to handle the situation properly.

#3 Know When to Leave the Scene

Some children can misunderstand what danger really is. If any conflict becomes physical, leave the area and report it to an adult.

#4 Follow the Examples of Those Around You

Your sense of good judgment comes from what you have seen and learned. Learn how to deal with conflicts by watching your parents, teachers, and older siblings deal with their conflicts.

WHEN NOT TO BE SOCIAL

An important part of engagement is knowing when to be social and when to avoid being social. This may seem pretty confusing, but it's true.

If you are alone or in a new environment where you barely know anyone, maintain a sense of security and be alert if you're talking to strangers. Take care not to share too much personal information with anyone until you know them well.

This also applies when you are in a place where people are involved in unkind or risky behaviors. You should know how to avoid such people, including fellow children.

There is an alarm center in your brain that can be activated when you are in a bad situation. If you start to feel unsafe, seek a way out of the situation immediately.

EVERYBODY'S DOING IT

Following trends is a major way to get lost to irresponsibility and low self-esteem. Part of developing social skills is learning how to deal with trends.

It's important to learn the value of contentment. Be confident in who you are and the abilities that you have. You should know that you are good enough and don't need to follow trends to make yourself feel included. Being up-to-date does not mean going along with all the trends, but rather being well-informed.

Have your own style. Think outside the box. This is not strange — it's unique! Just because everyone else is doing something does not mean it's the right thing to do.

You can talk with your parents or trusted adults about which trends you might want to follow, and which are inappropriate. These adults can help you to determine what feels right for you.

POSITIVE AND NEGATIVE PEER PRESSURE

Your peers have a major role to play in your development. This is because you spend a lot of time with them, and we are all naturally influenced by those around us.

Your peers can help you become the best version of yourself, and this is what we hope our friends will do. However, sometimes peers also pressure us to do things that don't feel quite right, or don't feel true to ourselves. Learn how to manage pressure from peers and how to weigh your options before giving in to anything that your peers ask you to do.

ACCEPTING POSITIVE PEER PRESSURE

Not all peer pressure is negative. Positive peer pressure encourages you to be better, challenge yourself, and try new things. The results of positive peer pressure are helpful and productive.

Your peers can influence you in a few ways, including:

- Forming study groups
- Learning new skills or an art
- Stopping a bad habit
- Exercising or playing sports
- Going to bed early
- Taking a break from phones
- Helping other kids
- Engaging in community service

The list is unending. You can influence your friends too, and you should open up to peer pressure that will help you to learn, grow, and improve over time.

What you think to be positive may not actually be positive, so make sure to discuss the suggestions your peers give you with your parents or a trusted adult.

RESISTING NEGATIVE PEER PRESSURE

Negative peer pressure is destructive. It often leads people to do things that don't feel right or comfortable to them, and can even be dangerous.

Know how to say NO when other kids in school or your neighborhood try to get you to do something that feels wrong to you.

You should know not to accept everything your friends say. Learn to talk to your parents or other adults like your teacher or school counselor about any incidents that make you confused or uncomfortable.

This means that there has to be healthy communication between you and your parents. Learn to open up to your parents and trust them.

You should know when to walk away when you are around bad kids and even take others with you. You can tell your friend, "Let's go—we have other things to do."

Choose your friends wisely. This is an important thing to do. If your friends don't do wrong things, then you probably won't either.

Talk to your parents about the peer pressure you face, whether it's positive or negative. If a child is trying to influence you negatively in school, ensure that you report that child to the school authorities immediately and to your parents when you get home.

DEALING WITH THE RUDE BEHAVIOR OF OTHERS

Rude behaviors can be so difficult to overlook, and when one person is rude, it can even tempt others to behave the same way. It's not clever to respond rudely to rude behavior. Instead, you can do any of the following:

#1 Be Kind

As impossible as it might seem, it is possible to be kind to a rude person. Sometimes, people are rude because they don't know how to keep their emotions in check and are unable to convey how they feel nicely.

Being kind protects you from catching the disease of rudeness. It also helps to leave a model for the rude person to emulate. The rude person may later reflect on their actions and look forward to communicating better next time.

#2 Call the Rude Person Out on Their Behavior

Learn to tell a rude child that they are being rude. If you are shy and want to turn away from a rude person immediately, encourage yourself to speak boldly, as long as your language and tone are polite.

FORGIVING OTHERS

Forgiveness is an important part of engagement. This is because, in the course of social interaction, people are bound to offend one another every now and then.

Forgiving others gives us a chance to be forgiven when we offend others too. It's important that you learn to let offenses go, especially when the offender makes an apology.

If you learn to forgive at a young age, you'll be able to handle adulthood more easily. Holding on to anger leads to bitterness, hatred, anxiety, and depression. It's to your own benefit to forgive.

Speak about how you feel about the offenders. You can say things like, "I did not like what you did or said, but I forgive you because it won't help me to hold on to anger." Learn to discuss your feelings with the offender or with others.

You can write a letter stating how you feel and stating that you forgive the offender. Then you can tear or burn the letter to signify that you are letting go of the negative feelings of anger.

You can even learn to forgive before an apology comes.

ACTIVITIES

Here are some activities that can help you develop your social skills:

#1

If you have difficulties expressing yourself, especially when you're talking with other kids or adults, write down the areas you struggle with and talk to your parents about it. They will give you advice on how you can improve.

Have conversations with your parents. Talk about topics you love. The more you talk about your favorite things with your parents and others you feel comfortable with (perhaps your siblings), the more you will eventually be able to engage well with others.

#2

Talk to your parents about struggles you face. Seek correction when you make mistakes, and practice this with others too.

#3

Make a list of everything that a friend has influenced you to do, and a list of things that you have influenced your friends to do. Show it or make it known to your parents so they can have an idea of your engagement with other kids and their influence on you.

Here's a game that also builds your engagement skills. You can suggest it to your teacher at school or play it at home with your family.

Charades

This game encourages everyone playing to participate. The person leading the game makes a list of different words. These words could be from a book on any subject.

Then, each player takes a turn standing in front of the others and acting out a word from the list. They can only act out the word; they shouldn't speak.

As they act out the word, the other players try to guess the word the actor is trying to demonstrate. Whoever gets the word can act out the next word. Keep going until you exhaust the topics on the list.

CHAPTE NINE:

SELF-CONTROL SKILLS

Self-control — this is a word that many people don't like to hear. It implies something tedious, or self-deprivation, but that's not what self-control has to be. Self-control applies in many if not all areas of our lives.

Self-control is the ability to stop yourself from doing or saying certain things when they are not healthy, appropriate, or productive. It's being able to control your desires or emotions so you don't end up doing things you will regret later. As difficult and impossible as it might sound, self-control isn't like that at all. You can learn to exercise a lot of self-control in different areas of your life and be the best you.

It's one thing to hear about self-control; it's another thing to actually exercise it. Thankfully, that's what this chapter is about. So come along and learn what self-control is all about and how to build this very important skill. You will also learn a thing or two about bullying and how you can handle it.

WHAT IS SELF-CONTROL?

In simple terms, self-control is the ability to control yourself — your emotions, desires, words, and behaviors. This means that you can tell yourself, "No, I won't do this," or "I won't do that," and then really follow through.

It also means you can manage your emotions and desire and not let them overwhelm you. For example, you're so angry and you have the perfect words to say that will hurt the other person. The ability to keep quiet and say nothing is self-control.

For another example, imagine your parent tells you not to play video games until 4pm. But then your parent leaves the house and you're so bored, so you think maybe you could just play one game. The ability to wait until 4pm is self-control. Or, you have to wait until after dinner before you can help yourself to some freshly baked chocolate-chip cookies. If you can pull through the delicious smell of the cookies and wait until after dinner, that's a lot of self-control.

So, you can see that many times in exercising self-control, you have to wait for the right time to do something even when you'd like to do it immediately.

WHY IS SELF-CONTROL IMPORTANT?

Self-control is actually one of the most important skills you can have, and its benefits are endless. With self-control, you'll be able to get more important things done and achieve your goals.

You can be a better student because you don't spend too many hours watching TV. You can be healthier because you don't eat all the sugar you want and you also eat more vegetables and do some exercise. You can feel well rested because you sleep when you should. You can even have more time for family because you're able to do your assignments and projects when they're meant to be done.

Add all this up, as little as each item may seem, and you're well on your way to being a person of excellent character. You'll also be healthy, dependable, and trustworthy.

Developing self-control helps you be more in charge of your emotions and feelings. It's easy to say really hurtful things when you're angry, things you can't take back because words stick. With self-control, you don't have to suffer such regrets.

Self-control will help you avoid many situations that lead to negative consequences. Sometimes these consequences can be life-changing. Sounds heavy? That goes to show just how important self-control is.

Another way to look at self-control is to think of it as discipline. When you exercise self-control, you'll become a disciplined person.

WHAT ARE EXAMPLES OF SELF-CONTROL?

By now, you're looking forward to having a lot of self-control. So, we'll show you some basic examples of self-control:

- Waiting your turn, no matter how long the line.
- Waiting patiently for everyone to come to the table before you eat.
- Doing your homework when you're told to or according to your schedule.
- Making a schedule and sticking to it.
- Not playing as many video games as you'd like.
- Learning to forgive those who hurt you and not pay them back in words or actions.

- Waiting for the right or best time before you do something.
- Not spending all the money that comes to you as gifts or allowance but instead saving some or using some to help others.
- Not blurting out secrets or surprises.

From the above examples, you can think up other ways to exercise self-control.

HOW DO I LEARN SELF-CONTROL?

Self-control comes naturally to some people, while for others it's more challenging to learn. Even so, for those it comes naturally to, there's always more to do.

So how can you become this person with a lot of self-control?

Prioritize: Learn to give different things their proper place in the order of importance. For example, have set times for having a bath, having an afternoon nap, eating lunch, doing your homework, and so on. Remember to plan time for play and leisure. Make sure you list your activities from the most important to the least.

Think before you speak: Learn not to say the first thing that comes to your mind. Instead, think about your words, especially when you're angry or excited, before you speak.

Take care of yourself: Eat right. Eat more vegetables and less sugar and sweets. Get enough sleep and exercise too. You should also avoid bad habits like biting your nails.

Make goals and stick with them: Break your goals into small pieces and give them time limits. Try to finish them up within the set time, and you'll find out you've done much more than you could imagine.

The need for self-control pops up in many situations, so watch out for these situations and apply self-control.

LEARNING TO REGULATE YOUR EMOTIONS

Emotions are the spice of life. Without them, life would be quite boring. However, sometimes emotions can feel like a roller coaster, so we need to have control over them. You must learn to put your emotions on a leash if you don't want them to run wild.

Regulating your emotions is not the same as suppressing them. Suppressing or ignoring emotions is very unhealthy. Rather, regulating your emotions means monitoring and controlling them so they don't get out of hand. It's about being able to dial down your emotions even when you're tempted to do something brash.

Imagine you didn't hear a complete conversation, but you think you might have heard someone criticize your appearance. Your mind might run away with this, feeling very upset and hurt, and in your anger you might say nasty things about those who you think criticized you. How do you think this will end when you find out that what you heard was not what was said? Now who's the real bully? It turned out to be you!

So, what do you do in situations like this, when you can feel your anger or other emotions starting to take hold?

Breathe. Yes, many things are going through your mind in that moment. Still, breathe deeply. Pause and don't do anything while you're upset. Wait a while till you're a bit more calm, and then ask questions.

Find out what was actually said by asking politely. You can say, "Hey, I happened to come in when you were talking with her. Did you say something about me?" Make sure you have all the facts before reacting, or overreacting.

Even if they did say something that was unkind, you don't need to internalize their opinion. Learn to be confident and not be moved by others' wrong opinions about you. You don't have to retaliate. It won't change what they already think about you; it will only worsen it.

So, to regulate your emotions, always pause and ask yourself: What am I feeling? Why am I feeling this way? How do I feel like reacting? Is this the best way to act? Usually, by the time you've finished answering these questions, you don't feel quite so strongly anymore. You've calmed down a bit.

It's the same with being very excited. You don't want to blurt out something you shouldn't at that time. So breathe, pause, and think. And you'll be fine.

HANDLING BULLIES

No one likes being bullied. However, many children have been bullied at times. You'll also be surprised to know that even adults get bullied sometimes. That's why you should learn how to handle bullies now so that it will be easier later.

What Is Bullying?

Bullying is when someone bigger or stronger tries to scare someone smaller or weaker. This is very wrong. The bigger person may try to hurt the smaller person physically or even harm the other person mentally through hurtful words. Bullying can happen anywhere, including at school.

Bullying can be very painful and depressing, which is why it's important to look out for it. Being bullied can lead to low self-esteem, fear, and isolation. You shouldn't let yourself be bullied. There are ways you can help stop a bully from taking advantage of you.

So how do you know you are being bullied? Let's look at the different types of bullying.

Types of Bullying

A person can be bullied in any of these ways:

Physically: This involves physical actions meant to hurt someone else's body, potentially involving hitting, bumping, or pinching.

Verbally: This involves using hurtful words to harm others.

Socially: This involves telling lies about a person and causing them to be avoided by their friends.

Social media: This involves using social media to embarrass or hurt someone, and it's a form of social bullying.

How to Respond to Bullies

Are you being bullied in any of these ways? How do you respond to it?

First, don't hide it. Tell someone older about it, so they know what to do.

Secondly, be bold.

Bullies like to go for people who seem small and weak, so stand strong. The best way to respond to bullies is to stand up for yourself.

Standing Up for Yourself

You don't actually have to be pushed around by a bully; stand up for yourself. Be confident in who you are, and don't let anymore make you feel less.

Once a bully sees that they can't threaten you, they will probably leave you alone.

Learn to ignore bullies. You don't really need to respond to everything they do. This is why you have to learn to regulate your emotions. You don't have to cry or feel scared in front of them. Let them see that their words or actions aren't affecting you and simply walk away.

In everything, be bold, be confident, and speak up. And don't delay in reporting bullies.

Don't be overly concerned about rumors and lies that spread around among your peers. Learn to trust in what is true and go with that. Also, find friends who will stick by you no matter what and be satisfied with those.

ACTIVITIES

We've compiled a list of games you can play to improve your self-control skills.

#1 Jenga

This is a game where you build a tower using wooden blocks. Each floor typically has three pieces, and each player takes turns to remove blocks from the tower. If the tower falls on your turn, you lose the game.

This game is great for practicing self-control as it requires slow and controlled movements. If you're too fast, the tower will come crashing down. The same thing happens if you fail to pay attention. You have to slow down and focus on winning this game.

#2 Red Light Green Light

You don't need any materials to play this game. Get a few friends and stand on one side of the room or playground. Select a leader to stand on the other side.

Once the leader says, "Green light," you all begin moving forward toward the leader. Then when the leader says, "Red light," everyone must freeze.

You can increase the level of hardness by changing the mandatory movements. The people who are moving could crab walk, hop, or bear crawl on the green light.

#3 Freeze Dance

Here's another game that you don't need materials for. Gather friends or family members together in an open space and begin to play music.

Everyone dances as long as the music is playing, but once the music stops, you must all freeze.

#4 Simon Says

In this game, you'll also select a leader who's in charge of giving instructions. The leader gives a directive like, "Raise your hands," but you can only follow the instruction if it begins with, "Simon says."

For instance, you shouldn't raise your hands if the leader says, "Raise your hands." You should only do so if they say, "Simon says, raise your hands."

CHAPTER TEN:

DESCISION-MAKING SKILLS

Decisions are a part of everyday life. Everyone makes decisions, except for tiny little babies. Everything you do is based on a decision you made. You choose to eat, wear clothes, play with your friends, respond when you are spoken to, etc. Basically, everything you do is a choice.

Everyone wants to be able to make the right choices. Sometimes, it can be hard to decide what clothes to wear, books to read, and friends to keep.

Decision-making skills are not only for adults to develop. You get to make decisions too, and there's a smart way to go about that. Skills are things you can learn. So, like every other skill, decision-making skills can be learned and developed.

In this chapter, we will discuss what decision-making is, and how you can make smarter decisions by having good decision-making skills. Let's jump right into it.

WHAT IS DECISION-MAKING?

Have you ever had to make a choice? Imagine that your mom bought two dolls, and you wanted the blonde one that your sister also wanted. What would you do in such a situation? Will you insist on the doll you want? Or will you let your sister have the blonde doll while you go for the dark-haired one?

You see, decision-making is the process of making a choice. It involves weighing your options to come up with the most suitable judgment. It's the process of having to choose the best option among all the alternatives that are available.

When making a decision, you look for the option that you like most or that is most beneficial. Sometimes, your judgment will be wrong, but that's fine. With practice and time, you will learn how to carefully think things through and decide on what is best for you and those around you. Eventually, you'll develop the ability to make the right decisions more often.

WHY ARE DECISION-MAKING SKILLS IMPORTANT?

Life revolves around choices. This means that everyone has to make decisions about a lot of things every day. Even choosing not to do something is a choice that you make. If you're patiently reading this book, it means you made a choice to read it.

Anything that will make you be the best version of yourself and will benefit those around you is essential. Decision-making skills help you develop your ability to think things through, explore ideas in your mind, and come up with a final and good result.

Proper decision-making skills do not aim at benefiting yourself only. With time, you will learn to consider other people when you are making decisions. This is because, often, the decisions you make will directly or indirectly affect other people.

Here are some reasons why you should develop your decision-making skills:

#1 Decision-Making Skills Earn You the Position of a Leader.

People want to be directed by someone who can make good decisions. In school, at home, and even on the playground with your friends, you will more likely be in charge of things if you are known to make good decisions.

#2 Decision-Making Skills Help You Be More Organized.

When you can make decisions about what to do, you will be able to carry out tasks in an organized manner. This is because you've already figured out what to do every time before you do it.

#3 Decision-Making Skills Will Help You Stay on Schedule.

Do you remember those times when you were late for school and missed the school bus? Or when you had to turn in your assignment or group project late? These things would not have happened if there had been proper decision-making about when to wake up, arrange your clothes for school, finish your project, and leave for school.

Decision-making skills give you control of your time and help you achieve tasks before they're due. That way, you'll avoid getting into unnecessary trouble. And in the future, it will help you achieve your goals.

#4 Decision-Making Skills Will Make You Trustworthy

When you are known for making good decisions, you can always be trusted by your parents, teachers and other adults to do the right things. This will help you be a confident and responsible adult when you grow up.

MAKING GOOD DECISIONS

We all make many decisions every day. Most decisions are easy, like what to have for breakfast. Regardless of what you decide, that decision is unlikely to have serious consequences. But some decisions are more important, and more difficult to make. It can be hard to know how to make a decision about an important topic, but the tips below will help you to do this.

#1 Try Not to Make a Decision When You Are Under Pressure

When you want to make a decision, ideally you should do so when you are calm and have time to think properly. If you are under pressure because you have a lot of assignments to do, or your friends want you to join them in doing something, it can be difficult to stay calm and make a smart decision.

Sometimes, you may need to pause and think about your decisions for a while, and that's okay. Don't be hasty, especially when there is no hurry. You don't want to make decisions that you will later regret.

For instance, don't insist that your parents buy you a particular dress for your birthday if your birthday is in a few months. This is because you may change your mind about the kind of birthday dress you want by that time. You should wait until a few weeks before the day to make a choice.

#2 Seek Advice From an Older Person

Older people have been your age before, and may have experienced similar situations. So they can be good people to go to for advice. When you want to decide what to do, you can always ask your parents or older siblings to guide you. If the decision is about making friends, talk to your parents about it.

#3 Think About All of Your Options Before Making a Decision

Don't be too quick to decide on something. Always consider multiple options. If you're taking a test and you're not sure which answer to pick, look through all of the options and think carefully about them before you make your choice.

If you're confused about what to do for your vacation, write down what options are available, think about the possible benefits of each choice, and pick the best choice there is.

#4 Think About How Your Decision Affects Others

This is a very important part of decision-making. Just like you don't want anyone's choices to hurt you, when you make your choices you must also try not to hurt others. Whenever you want to make a decision, think of the people your decision will affect and let that be a major factor in the choice you make.

For example, some children have stayed back from going on a trip just so that they could be with their sick siblings who would be home alone without them. Thinking about others when you make decisions will help you to be kind, and will help others to know that you are reliable and compassionate.

GETTING MORE INFORMATION BEFORE MAKING A DECISION

You must get enough information about something before making an informed decision.

If you want to attend a friend's party and need to decide what to wear, first you should know what kind of party it is. Is it a birthday party? Or a costume party?

When you know what kind of party it is, you should ask if everyone is expected to dress a certain way. This will help you decide what to wear.

After you have decided what to wear, find out the time for the party and the place. Knowing the time and place will help you decide when to dress up and leave the house.

This can also apply if you have an assignment or project to do in school. You should inquire about the type of project you will be working on, the materials required, and the deadline for submission. This will help you decide where to get the materials and when to begin your project.

Always ask questions and find out more things before you decide to do anything. A little information is not enough; make sure you have enough to make an informed decision.

HEAD VERSUS HEART DECISIONS:

Decisions can be made either from the heart or the head, and you may find that you make different kinds of decisions in different situations.

Head Decisions

Head decisions are decisions you make based on careful thought. When you make decisions from your head, you are allowing yourself to consider different options carefully without any rush or emotional attachment, and to try to come to the decision that makes the most logical sense or seems most practical.

Heart Decisions

Heart decisions are decisions made based on how you feel — happy, sad, angry, excited, or any other emotions. At these moments, you might not be calm, which makes it difficult to think about things carefully. The best time to make decisions is when we are calm, because it's easier then to think through all of the facts and possible consequences.

LEARNING THAT NOT EVERYTHING IS A CRISIS

A crisis is an unstable moment when everything seems to be falling apart. It's a moment when you are afraid, anxious, or worried because you are scared of something negative happening.

Making decisions should not make you worried, scared, or nervous. Just because you're not sure what decision to make doesn't always mean there is a crisis. Many times, what you're worried about is probably not a very big deal. If you understand this, you will be able to stay calm when you're worried.

Staying calm will help you make more rational decisions. This is because you will be able to rationally think through the situation and arrive at the best outcome.

When you are in a situation where you don't know what to do, and you are scared and worried, look for an older person (such as your parent or teacher) and talk to them about how you feel. Don't be hasty to make any decisions at this point. Make sure you are calm before deciding anything.

WHAT IS COMMON SENSE?

Common sense is cleverness in simple matters. You can make a good judgment after thinking things through. Common sense is used when decisions need to be made over small matters. Common sense helps you to do the most natural, simple, and rational thing in any situation.

When you return from school, it's common sense to put your clothes in the laundry basket and put your shoes on the rack. It's also common sense to take a bath after every sports game or after swimming in a lake.

Common sense is a smart thing that comes naturally. You learn to have common sense by observing those around you and how well they do things. When you are corrected about wrongdoing, you gain common sense; you learn from your mistakes and do not repeat them.

USING YOUR COMMON SENSE

You don't need to be working on a difficult homework assignment to use your common sense. Common sense is used every day in everything you do.

When speaking to an older person, common sense teaches you not to be rude but to talk politely. When you get up or wake up in the morning, common sense tells you to greet your parents and older siblings, brush your teeth, and take a shower.

Common sense will help you make the right decision every day.

QUESTIONS TO ASK YOURSELF

A few questions can help you know how well developed your decision-making skills are and whether you use your common sense correctly.

- Am I scared when I have a lot of things to do?
- Do I finish my tasks (e.g., assignments, chores) on time?
- Am I always late for school, parties, activities, or appointments?
- What do I do when I wake up every day?
- How do I act when I am happy or sad?
- Do I think about my decisions before I make them?

ACTIVITIES

#1

If you are always late for school or late in submitting an assignment, or if you seldom finish what you have to do before the time is up, here's something that can help you:

- Write a list of things you have to do on a piece of paper.
- Get another piece of paper and arrange your list according to what you want to do first, second, third, etc.
- Write out the time it will take you to finish each task and get to work.

#2

If you have a hard time deciding what to wear, you can spend your weekends arranging your clothes for the week. Sort out which clothes you want to wear for each day. Do the same for your shoes.

#3

Go through the list of how to make good decisions and put them into practice every day for a week. Record what your results are and show them to your parents or older sibling.

Tic Tac Toe

This game, also called naughts and crosses, is a great game to practice your decision-making skills. In this game, you'll need to choose squares that'll help you get a row of three. But that's not all. You also need to choose squares that stop your partner from getting three in a row.

Here's how you play the game:

- Draw an outline of two vertical lines and two horizontal lines intersecting them, forming nine squares.
- Each player should choose a symbol (one should be zeroes, the other crosses).
- Take turns placing your mark (0 or X) in an open square.
- To win, you must make a row (vertical, horizontal, or diagonal) with your symbol.

CHAPTER ELEVEN:

RESPECT SKILLS

You have probably heard people say to you, "Show some respect" or "Have some respect." This might be confusing, especially if you don't know what they are asking you to do.

You might feel this way because you don't quite know what the word respect means. To understand what respect means or stands for, you first need a proper definition.

When you understand what respect is all about, then you'll be able to practice it.

Learning and practicing respect skills will help you in getting along with people from different places.

This chapter will consider what respect means and why it's important, as well as the areas where it applies. The goal of this chapter is primarily to help you learn respect skills and when you would need to apply them.

WHAT IS RESPECT?

Respect is an important part of our everyday life. The term respect comes from the Latin word *respectus* which means consideration, regard, or attention. Simply put, respect has to do with the value, honor, or esteem a person has for another individual or for an object or idea.

Specifically, respect could also mean accepting people for who they are, even if they are different from you in terms of their beliefs, opinions, or views. Respect can come in two forms: respect as an attitude and respect as a behavior.

Respect as an attitude plays out in your thoughts toward an individual, idea, or object. On the other hand, respect as a behavior has to do with demonstrating the respect you have for a person, idea, or object through your words as well as your actions.

WHY ARE RESPECT SKILLS IMPORTANT?

There are several reasons why respect is important and worth learning. Practicing respect will help shape the way you think of others and how you treat them.

Below are some reasons why you should learn respect skills:

#1 Good Relationships with Others

You can only build good relationships with others when you have respect for them. If you don't have respect skills, you may find it difficult to become friends with people around you. This is because many people are unwilling to talk with someone they find disrespectful. In fact, being around such a person often leads to misunderstandings or hurt feelings.

#2 Effective Communication

In most cases, communication can only continue if both people involved respect each other and as a result, they listen and try to understand one another. When you communicate respectfully, it will be easier for you to achieve whatever you have in mind.

#3 Open-Mindedness and Fairness

Respect skills guide you not to disregard any opinions, ideas, values, and beliefs that differ from yours. Instead, you will learn to accept the differences that exist between you and others and to consider them without being partial.

#4 Ability to Easily Make Friends

Respect skills help you to remember that everyone is a valuable member of society. These skills also help you to honor the opinions, beliefs, and values of others. Consequently, they will enable you to have good relationships with all different kinds of people.

#5 Tolerance

This is related to #4 above. In the course of your daily life, you are likely to come across people that have ideas, opinions, or beliefs that are different from yours. You might not always agree with them, but having respect skills will help you to be tolerant when addressing these differences.

#6 Civility/Good Manners

Respect is the foundation for good manners. It's nearly impossible to have good manners without showing respect. For example, showing respect to someone usually appears through being polite to them.

#7 Willingness to Learn

Respect skills create the willingness to learn. This is because when you have respect skills, you will place value on what other people have to say. For instance, you would not take whatever your teacher or your parents have to say for granted.

#8 Quality of Life

If you want to live a good and happy life, it's important that you acquire respect skills. Specifically, respect skills will help you in creating good relationships with people who will be willing to help you when the need arises.

GETTING ALONG WITH YOUR PARENTS

You probably spend a lot of time with your parents, and hopefully you will continue to do so throughout your life. As you know, relationships go most smoothly when everyone shows each other respect and makes an effort to get along.

To get along with your parents, there are some things you must do:

#1 Be Attentive to Your Parents

This means listening well. Being attentive to your parents can go a long way when trying to get along with them. This is because when you are attentive to their requests or instructions, it shows that you value and respect them. Also, attentiveness allows you to learn things that you wouldn't have known otherwise.

#2 Seek Their Permission

Whenever you are planning on doing something, it's important you let your parents know and seek their permission. Doing this will make sure that you don't perform any action that will be unsafe or displease your parents.

#3 Don't Be Rude While Expressing Yourself

You will often run into problems with your parents when you speak to them rudely. If you want to get along with your parents, you should ensure that you are polite in the way you address them. While speaking to your parents, you can use phrases such as, "Please," "May I," and "Excuse me." This tip goes for your interactions with everyone, not just your parents.

#4 Carry Out Assigned Tasks

If you want to get along with your parents, it's important that you always carry out the tasks they assign to you. This could mean keeping your room tidy, feeding your family dog, or watering the flowers.

In a situation where you don't like the task your parents have given you, talk to them about it instead of refusing to do it. Talking to them about it may result in them changing the task.

#5 Take Responsibility

If you have done something wrong to offend your parents, you shouldn't give excuses or blame someone else. In this situation, apologize and take full responsibility for your actions.

#6 Follow Their Instructions

One of the major reasons why it may be difficult to get along with your parents is a result of failing to follow their instructions. It's a good idea to follow your parents' instructions because they give these instructions out of love and care and not as a way of punishing you.

GETTING ALONG WITH SIBLINGS

There are many ways for you to get along with your siblings. However, your success in this area depends greatly on the respect skills you have learned.

Here are the different ways to get along with your siblings:

#1 Respect Each Other's Differences

Understanding how your siblings differ from you is the first step in getting along with them. This means that they may not have the same likes and dislikes as you.

For instance, you may prefer watching a particular movie while your siblings may like another. Instead of fighting in such a situation, you and your siblings can take turns watching your favorite movies.

This shows that you respect each other's differences and will not force them into liking the same things as you.

#2 Understand That You Are Equal

It would be difficult to have a good relationship with your siblings if you believe that you are better than them and deserve to be treated better.

Having a cordial relationship with your siblings requires you to see them as equals. When you see your siblings as equals, you won't disregard their opinion or whatever they say to you. This ensures fairness for all.

#3 Offer to Teach Your Siblings

Teaching your siblings can go a long way in helping you get along with them. For instance, you can try to teach your sibling to ride a bike, solve a puzzle, or play a video game. This is a great way to use your own skills and knowledge for the benefit of others, and gives you and your siblings a good chance to spend time and cooperate together.

#4 Avoid Being Mean to Your Siblings

If you want to get along well with your siblings, you must avoid being mean to them. Being mean could involve speaking rudely to your sibling or taking something that belongs to them.

No matter what your sibling might have done to offend you, you should try not to act mean as a way of getting back at them. Instead, you can try to discuss the problem and find a solution together. If you're not able to do so, your parents might be able to help.

#5 Forgive Your Siblings

All siblings argue sometimes. The goal isn't to avoid this entirely, but rather to avoid unnecessary arguments and to learn how to recover from them quickly. When your sibling offends you, you should let them know what they did that made you unhappy and subsequently forgive them. However, if your sibling continues doing the same thing to offend you, you should inform your parents about it.

#6 Share Your Things with Your Siblings

You can share your personal belongings with your siblings. Doing this will strengthen the bond between you. Nevertheless, you can set some rules about sharing your things. For instance, you could establish the rule that they inform you before using your personal belongings.

GETTING ALONG WITH TEACHERS AND AUTHORITY FIGURES

The importance of respecting authority figures cannot be taken for granted. Authority figures include parents, teachers, mentors, community leaders, and government officials.

To an extent, authority figures play an important role in ensuring that people act in the right way, and hopefully in ways that are fair and good for everyone. People like your parents and teachers are there to help you learn and grow safely, and listening to them is in your best interest.

Here are the various ways to get along with authority figures:

#1 Understand the Importance of Each Authority Figure

Each authority figure plays a different role. When you understand these roles, it will be easier for you to get along with them.

For instance, while in the classroom, the role of your teacher is to guide you through the learning process and to impart knowledge. Knowing this will encourage you to pay attention to every instruction your teacher gives.

In contrast, the role of a police officer is to ensure safety and that laws are followed. So you won't look to a police officer to necessarily impart knowledge to you, but you'll obey what they say to ensure the safety and order of your community.

#2 Speak Politely to Authority Figures

If you really want to be on good terms with an authority figure, you must be polite in the way you speak to them and in your actions. When addressing them, make use of phrases such as "Thank you," "Yes ma'am/No ma'am," or "Yes sir/No sir."

#3 Give an Apology When Appropriate

Whenever you have gone against the instructions of an authority figure, you should take responsibility for your actions and apologize. Also, you should inform them that you will make amends for your actions.

RESPECTING THE PROPERTY OF OTHERS

When we refer to others' property, we refer to anything that belongs to them. This could be your friend's bike, your sister's soccer ball, or your dad's favorite book. These objects are not yours, so you must treat them with respect.

When dealing with other people's property, ask yourself the question, "How would I feel if someone damaged my property?" For example, "How would I feel if someone lost my soccer ball?" or "How would I feel if someone ripped my favorite book?" If you know that those things would upset you, then assume they will upset others as well, and be sure to treat their property with care.

Also, respecting other people's property means asking for their permission before making use of what belongs to them and never taking anything that does not rightfully belong to you.

DEMONSTRATING GOOD MANNERS TOWARD OTHERS

Demonstrating good manners is something that you should learn. This is because it helps a lot when trying to have a good relationship with the people you meet.

Maintaining a good relationship with others will often make people consider you to be someone special and someone who they will be willing to help if need be.

Here are some ways you can demonstrate good manners:

Use phrases such as, "Thank you," "May I," "Please," and "Excuse me," when communicating with other people.

You should greet your friends and family whenever they arrive, including those who you are meeting for the first time.

Speak to other people only in the way you want others to speak to you.

Always wait for your turn whenever you are communicating with someone or performing a task that involves other people.

Avoid making use of offensive words while communicating with others.

ACTIVITIES

Here are some fun activities that encourage respect skills:

In your own words, describe what respect means and then try to recall any situation in the past where you acted respectfully.

List out your superheroes and write down the respectful things they did, maybe in a movie or a comic book.

Starting this week, every day give someone a genuine compliment. When you get home, write down the person who you gave the compliment and their reaction.

Watch a television show and try to determine who was respectful and who was not.

Imagine someone older than you yelled at you for something you never did. What would be your response? Or how would you react? Write down your answer.

List three ways you feel you can show your parents respect.

List three ways you can show your teachers that you respect them.

CHAPTER TWELVE:

EMPATHY

How you act with your friends and loved ones matters a lot. It'll either get your friends to cherish you more or lead people to avoid you.

This is because people tend to react according to how you make them feel. If they tend to feel threatened and misunderstood around you, they'll be uncomfortable when you're present.

So, knowing how to treat people is important, whether it's your sibling, family friend, schoolmate, or a complete stranger. You can train yourself to always behave in a way that makes others feel comfortable around you. This skill is what we call empathy.

So, what does empathy look and sound like? That's what this chapter is going to explain.

WHAT IS EMPATHY?

We're all born selfish. Think about it. As a child, you'd cry anytime and anywhere. You didn't care if it was the middle of the night or if your parents were incredibly tired. All you cared about was yourself.

As you grew, this trait didn't just vanish. You had to be taught to consider the feelings of others. So, you learned to not disturb your parents when they're busy or having a rough day.

That's what empathy is. It's being able to understand another person's feelings or emotions. When you have empathy skills, you can see things from the point of view of others and place yourself in their shoes.

Simply put, if you're empathetic, you'll be aware of other people's feelings and know how to respond in certain situations.

WHY IS EMPATHY IMPORTANT?

The world would be a better and more loving place if everyone showed a little more kindness. Empathy is crucial if you want to have positive friendships and relationships. With empathy skills, you can avoid misunderstandings and conflict.

Here are some reasons why learning empathy is crucial:

It teaches you to value every person, regardless of their background, gender, or race.

It helps you to control and develop your emotions. You'll come to understand that wanting something does not mean that you'll always get it. This will shield you from vices like envy and jealousy.

Empathy skills help you know not to bully others. This is because you learn that you should do to others only what you want to be done to you.

Learning about empathy helps you act in more mature ways. You'll find it easier to identify ways to help others.

It builds stronger friendships. When you empathize with your friends, it shows that you value and care for them.

The more you practice putting yourself in another person's shoes, the more you learn to be grateful and appreciate your things.

Empathy helps you be a better individual as a whole. You will learn to respect other people's personal space.

HOW CAN YOU BUILD EMPATHY?

Like building a muscle, you develop empathy through constant practice. Here are a few things you can do to help build your empathy skills:

1. Talk about your feelings.

When things happen, talk about them with your friends and family. When you feel hurt or sad, rather than holding it inside, talk to someone you trust about your feelings.

2. Watch the grown-ups.

Look at what your parents or trusted older people do to help others. For example, what did your mother do when her friend was sick? Pay attention to the words they say and how they act.

3. Don't be a sore loser.

Learn the habit of good sportsmanship. Know that you won't always win at everything. It's okay to lose sometimes. When that happens, you should celebrate with the winner. Maybe next time, with enough hard work, it'll be your turn to win.

4. Always consider the feelings of others.

Know that other people have emotions too, even when you can't tell how they're feeling. If you felt bad over something that happened, that's the same way others may feel in that situation. So, before you do something, think about how you'd feel if another person did that to you.

5. Learn to observe body language.

We've already seen that people communicate both verbally and nonverbally. To empathize with others, you must learn to identify how they feel even when they don't say anything.

6. Interact with people from different backgrounds and cultures.

This will help broaden your perspective. It will also help you see that being different is okay.

7. Respect personal space and boundaries.

Overall, respect the boundaries of others. If a person says they're not comfortable with a game or action, don't ignore them. Instead, respect their decision.

ACTIVITIES

Now you know what empathy means and why it's important. Let's identify some fun activities you can do to grow your empathy skills.

1. Read stories or watch movies and then discuss the characters.

After reading a novel or seeing a movie, talk with your friends or family members about the characters. Discuss the emotions of the characters. What did they feel, believe, and want?

Also, talk about what you'd have thought, felt, or done in similar situations.

2. Do volunteer work.

Volunteering your time is a great way to help out with something you care about in your community. You can even start a project or charitable organization to solve a problem you feel strongly about.

3. Register for acting classes.

Stepping into character will help you feel what it's like to be in a particular situation.

FINAL WORDS

Finally! You've successfully finished reading the entire book. This is no small feat, so congratulations!

However, you must decide to put these lessons into practice. That's how you grow. As you practice the skills we've discussed in this book, you'll begin to experience their benefits.

Remember to be patient with yourself. Rome wasn't built in a day. Likewise, you won't suddenly become socially adept in one sitting. But with constant practice and patience, you'll get there.

Made in United States
Orlando, FL
16 December 2022

26804597R00085